# Commonplace Book, 1934–2012

Quotations (Books, Articles, Reviews, Letters), Recollections (Persons, Places, Events), Words (Archaic, Obsolescent, Technical), including Story Plots, Fancies, Sententiae, Verse, and Nonsense

**Daniel Aaron**

Pressed Wafer: BROOKLYN

**Pressed Wafer**
375 Parkside Avenue, Brooklyn, NY 11226
www.pressedwafer.com

ISBN 978-1-940396-12-5
FIRST EDITION
Printed in the United States

*Ubi nihil erit quod scribas, id ipsum scribito.*
CICERO, Epistolae ad Atticum

*The friends that have it I do wrong*
*Whenever I remake a song,*
*Should know what issue is at stake:*
*It is myself that I remake.*
W. B. YEATS

*A book wherein I write everything, as I see it or as*
*thoughts suggest it to me …*
G. C. LICHTENBERG

*Each alone on the heart of the earth,*
*impaled upon a ray of sun:*
*and suddenly it's evening.*
SALVATORE QUASIMODO

*Isn't it wonderful how we continue to be distracted,*
*nay obsessed, by trivia until we expire. I know that*
*while alive I must yield to the pull of a pretty shape*
*or face. It is a heliotropic response. Here I am at 93*
*responding like a schoolboy to a charming gesture,*
*only now I savor the charm more intensely and*
*knowledgeably than ever before.*
SIR CHARLES TENNYSON

*I saw an unscrewed spider spin a thought*
*And walk away upon the wings of angels.*
Nathaniel Lee

*… novels will give way, by and by, to diaries or*
*autobiographies;—captivating books, if only a man*
*knew how to choose among his experiences that which*
*is really his experience, and how to record truth truly.*
R. W. Emerson

*Rest? Rest? Shall I not have all Eternity to rest in?*
Thomas Carlyle

*Why let our living be a cheap and broken hour, which*
*should be an affluent eternity?*
Henry David Thoreau

*Daniel could be better liking with pulse than others*
*were with the Kings dainties.*
William Bradford, Of Plymouth Plantation

*[Arnold Schoenberg] was so number sensitive that*
*he went so far as to spell "Aron" with only one A, so*
*there would be only 12 letters in the title of his opera,*
Moses und Aron.
David Huckvale, The Occult Arts of Music

*There is a story that Stephen Tennant was the product of Dr. Aaron, who had a method of artificially inseminating society women who could not conceive with their husbands. In one version, the doctor had a stud of eligible footmen waiting outside the door. In another, a teaspoon was used to carry the husband's semen to impregnate his wife.*

PHILIP HOARE, Serious Pleasures: The Life of Stephen Tennant

*If I had a friend to advise in early life I should say, "change your name to Aaron," and you will be pretty safe to head all alphabetical lists.*

SAMUEL BUTLER

**Commonplace Book**

Story of a cleric, captured by the Saracens. They keep piercing him with arrows. "How do you like that?" they ask him—to which he gives no answer. Then they chop off his head. "How do you like that?" The head replies: "I like it very well."

## On Criticism

*Machiavelli to Francesco Vettori*: "That a man should never be rebuked when he knows that he is in the wrong: this only serves to increase his suffering and not to cure or lessen his error."

"I never say what I believe nor believe what I say, and if I sometimes tell the truth I conceal it among so many lies that it is not easy to discover it."

*John Locke*: "Who is there hardy enough to contend with the reproach which is everywhere prepared for those who dare venture to dissent from the received opinions of their country or party? And where is the man to be found that can patiently prepare himself to bear the name of whimsical, skeptical, or atheist, which he is sure to meet with, who does in the least scruple any of the common opinions?"

"The floating of other men's opinions in our brains makes us not one jot the more knowing, though they happen to be true."

## Story Idea: Movie Night

At the movie last night, the maniac raised a horrid mace-like tool and gibbered imprecations. Even the lady detective, who was seldom perturbed, glanced about uneasily. It was evident that her maddened adversary intended to bash her on the head—just as he had done to the girl and her old father.

As the family retainer cackled in anticipation of a blood-feast, I glanced nervously around and watched a little boy in the row behind me slowly climb out of his seat. He was badly frightened but couldn't take his eyes off something so terrible and wild. His cheeks were drawn and the cords of his neck slightly distended.

The madman swung at the lady detective two or three times before he crashed through the banister and plunged three flights. The boy sank back into his seat and whispered furtively to a friend next to him. What momentous shapes must have tormented him that night. Perhaps the dream-boy is running through a green jungle, home of insatiable shadows, the shrubs part, and the boy sees the madman, thrice terrible in dream costume, and the chase begins. The boy runs and runs and runs; the demon thumps inexorably behind him. But then the boy stumbles. The Shape runs him down, and the boy shrieks himself awake.

"The sentimentalists are practical men who believe in money, in position, in a marriage bell, and whose understanding of happiness is to be so busy whether at work or at play, that all is forgotten but the momentary aim."

*Episcopalians*: "Their worship is so cold and formal, that a few of their prayer-books thrown into Hell would freeze it over, so that the Devil would have good skating."

*Unitarians*: "Their steeples should point downward, in order to give a correct idea of where the people are bound."

## Neologisms

"Boatable," "anti-fogmatic," "helliniferous,"
"neat as plush," "go-betweenity," "carniverosity,"
"I rather expect," "I don't know but you might,"
"strengthy," "a little bit ago."

*Sunday, Sept. 22:* This is the month when house-keepers are complaining about the Office of Price Administration while they crush you against meat counters. Henry Wallace has been removed from the cabinet; the newspapers become increasingly bellicose about Russia and the "new appeasement." This is the time when gray flan-nels cost $15 and up, when people are camping in miserable surroundings (and with relatives), when help is hard to find and nerves are frazzled. The Dodgers and the Cards are making a photo finish.

To take incidents from a biographical sketch of W. D. Howells and to work them into a ghost story à la E. T. A. Hoffmann. Howells, the timid son of solid loving mother, Sherwood Andersonian grandpa, Swedenborgian poppa. Other characters include Centre Claws with iron talons radiating from his stomach, Irishman Dowd (who wears iron spectacles), Solomon Whistler (crazed after being drafted into the War of 1812).

## On Imagination

*Émile Faguet:* "In a being who is helpless in action, imagination takes the place and does the work of other faculties, moulding matter, traveling to the ends of the world, building palaces, planting rocks, opening avenues and creating the universe which desire demands."

"Mysterious East"

The Emir of Tashkent,
Wondering where his cash went,
Suspected his cousin,
And after him, the Muezzin,
Until he remembered that an uncle in Transjordia
Had kleptomania.

## An Afternoon with Sinclair Lewis

*April 16*: Join Day Tuttle (Smith College theater department), who has planned a visit to South Williamstown to discuss dramatization of *Kingsblood Royal*. We arrive at "Thorvale" (large spacious white house inside 800 acres of hilly land at the base of the Taconic Trail).

Lewis asleep when we arrive. A Mrs. Powers, white-haired and alert, lets us in. We go into a large living room with a splendid view of Mt. Greylock and long running fields. Enter Lewis: tall and gangling, shuffling walk. Thin wisps of yellow-white hair, combed back, large red patch on the right side of his face, marked palsy. A copy of Anaïs Nin's book on his living room table, shelves of records, a set of the Nonesuch Dickens. Lewis is proud of his house and obviously enjoys his possessions.

We take a walk through a beautiful birch grove. I ask him if Veblen had influenced him. (No, he'd never read him.) Mrs. Powers had whisky laid out for use on our return. Lewis, now a reluctant teetotaler, doesn't enjoy watching others drink.

Yeats and Keats, his favorite poets.

Sherwood Anderson largely a fake. (I challenge him and compare Anderson to Whitman.) "Whitman is a 'fake' too," he replies. Describes a mellow evening with Eugene Debs and Carl Sandburg in West Side Chicago, Debs—the romantic, the lovely soul—getting wildly high and describing how the railroad dicks would follow him from train to train, and how he could always spot them before inviting them to sit with his conductor and fireman friends near the stove to keep warm.

Some reminiscences of his father doctor, of Upton Sinclair and Helicon Hall; his dislike of Yale architecture; his fondness for the writers of the 1890s (Harold Frederic, Hamlin Garland); his son Wells Lewis (whom I knew at Harvard). Says he should have been a Methodist exhorter. Likes to win, enjoys violence and enthusiasms, distrusts silent people who have no strong likes and dislikes. Quickly called me Dan and said he'd remember "Aaron" since it was the first name of the hero in his next book—a historical novel about life in Minnesota in the 1840s (missionaries, Calvinism, etc.). He wants to visit Northampton and meet our friends and wives. Eager for more talk.

**True & False**

*Pascal*: "When the word of God, which is really true, is false literally, it is true spiritually."

> *Thomas Paine*: "Infidelity does not consist in believing or disbelieving; it consists in professing to believe what he does not believe."

## Fewer Brutes

*Hippolyte Taine*: "Intimacy with great writers enables us to multiply those quarter houses in which one is not entirely a brute."

## The Colossal Error

*Flaubert to George Sand, August 3, 1870*: "I am mortified with disgust at the stupidities of my country-men. The irremediable barbarity of mankind fills me with a bitter melancholy. Their wild enthusiasm, prompted by no intelligent motive, makes me long to die, that I may be spared the sight of it."

"Perhaps there will be a return to racial wars, and within the next century we shall see millions of men killing one another in a single action, all the East against all Europe, the old world against the new."

"Mankind is indeed far from the ideal of its cultured folks. Our colossal and tragic error is to suppose it to be like ourselves and to treat it accordingly."

## DA on Hawthorne and Sin

Not so much Christian as Romantic & Faustian.
But it's also Calvinistic or Edwarsdian. The doomed
are wrapped up in themselves, isolated from
God. This is the real terror of Edwards' Hell.
Evil equals dissonance.

## A Thought on the Dead

A dead man is alone when he is dead and more alone when he is forgotten. I should like to renew my friendship with the dead, to think of them frequently and to speak to them. And I should like people to think of me in that way when I am dead. I hope I shall be available to my children and to my surviving friends and they will think of me in a friendly way when they are having a good time.

Freud describes his elation as he stands on the
Acropolis and looks out over the blue sea. What
they told him at school is really true, and for
him this is really an important *Aha-Erlebnis*.
"Oh miracle of geography! Oh glorious confir-
mation that Paris really exists and that the long
Finnish peninsula juts into the Baltic!"

## Making Sin Ridiculous

Martin Marprelate—pen name for group of anonymous pamphleteers (1588) who satirized Presbyterian ecclesiastics. Charged with making sin ridiculous instead of odious, Marprelate replies: "Aye, for jesting is lawful by circumstances, even in the highest matters . . . The Lord being the author of both mirth and gravity, is it not lawful in itself for the Truth to use either of these ways?"

## The Great Secret Enemy

*Re: Presidential Election*: Eisenhower's popularity with women, corruption, press-agentry, personal glamour, desire for change. Inertia. The reassuring Father (stern, kindly, yet boyish) will protect USA from the Great Secret Enemy. "Dick" Nixon is Veep.

## How to Respond to Writers Who Do Not Read

Dr. Samuel Johnson's reply to the poison-pen Hugh Kelly, who had apologized for prolonging a visit that might have been troublesome: "Not in the least, sir. I had forgotten you were in the room." Johnson referred to Kelly as "a man who had written more than he had read."

**On Bad History**

Johnson on the historian William Robertson,
who painted minds the way [Sir Joshua] Reynolds
imagined "heroic countenances." SJ likened
him to "a man who has packed gold in the wool;
the wool takes up more room than the gold . . .
I would say to Robertson what an old tutor of
college said to one of his pupils, 'Read over your
compositions, and, whenever you meet with
a passage which you think is particularly fine,
strike it out.'"

**Story Idea: The Plagiarist**

A young unattached teacher in a women's college
lectures to his classes every year on the criminal
practice of using others' words without acknowl-
edgment. He can invariably spot such pilferings,
he tells them, and warns of the dire consequences.
Then (as he predicts) one student tries it. She is
a sulky girl with a certain prettiness but disgrun-
tled and soiled looking, quite unlike the clean
rosy-cheeked Dianas he prefers. Puzzled at first,
teacher turns detective and discovers the telltale
source of the plagiarism—two or three sentences
lifted from a 1943 review in the *New Republic*.
His fiendish delight at her exposure. The con-
frontation scene and his embarrassment and
lame rejoinder to her brazen self-defense.

## The Right Sort of Happiness

*From* Pride and Prejudice: "To his wife he was very little otherwise indebted, than as her ignorance and folly had contributed to his amusement. This is not the sort of happiness which a man would in general wish to owe to his wife; but where other powers of entertainment are wanting, the true philosopher will derive benefit from such as are given."

". . . how little of personal happiness could belong to a couple who were only brought together because their passions were stronger than their virtue, she could easily conjecture."

## Formic Bliss

*From a Book about Ant Behavior:* "In the middle of a hill in an air-conditioned chamber completely dark lives the queen of the white ants. She lays 30 eggs a minute night and day every day in all seasons, and the male ant never leaves her."

## Robert Kennedy and the Warsaw Entourage

He was said to be ruthless and arrogant. His
association with Sen. Joseph McCarthy is a black
mark. RK and his entourage had paid a destructive visit to Warsaw shortly before I got there.
My friends in the Embassy there told me that
he had harangued the populace from the tops
of embassy cars and disrupted official business
for a month.

Note how the Baconian axiom "knowledge is power" becomes a hallmark in America: it sanctifies the pragmatic, the utilitarian. But our writers (Emerson, Thoreau, Whitman, Melville, Hawthorne, James) divide those who have "lived" from those immured in a "pig lead" world. Perhaps the chief value of the American religious heritage is its counter-materialism. Church and religion were bound to be tarnished by American materialism, to become at times adjuncts of business. Still, Christian doctrines have reminded Americans of something beyond hard realities. Jonathan Edwards attacked easy complacent virtues—the hypocrisy of the moral sense.

*Ronald Knox*: "But indeed that American soil is an ever-generous mother to the faiths which are implanted there."

America ... "that land of exaggeration."

"At the heart of him, the Evangelist is always an experimentalist. He feels certain that something has happened to him, and he invites you to let it happen to you—that is, really, the whole of his message."

## On Learning

What joy to learn—more satisfying than love, yet
all the better when pursued in the aura of love.

## The Manias of History

*Marc Bloch*: "So in many cases the demon of origins has been, perhaps, only the incarnation of the other satanic enemy of true history: the mania for making judgments."

"With some reason, perhaps, the man of the age of electricity and of the airplane feels himself far removed from his ancestors. With less wisdom, he has been disposed to conclude that they have ceased to influence him."

"It is advisable and, in my opinion, it is indispensable that the historian possess at least a smattering of all the principal techniques of his trade, if only to learn the strength of his tools and the difficulties of handling them."

"Today we should no longer dare to say without qualification that literature 'is the expression of society.' That is by no means true—at least not in the sense that a mirror is the 'expression' of the object which it reflects. Literature may as easily express a defense reaction to its society as an acceptance of it. Almost inevitably, it carries along a great number of inherited themes, of formal devices learned in the study, of outworn æsthetic conventions, which act as so many causes of retardation."

## Tomorrow's Audience

A man living circa 1953 writes a letter to his yet unborn posterity. On Sunday nights, he tells them, the radios hummed with dramas of murder and violent crime, and a still churchgoing people fed on grisly deeds. After every bloodbath, radio audiences were enjoined to remember that crime doesn't pay.

### "Thro' the World" with Blake

It is right it should be so
Man was made for Joy & Woe
And when this we rightly know
Thro' the World we safely go.

## The Difficulty of History

*Matthew Paris*: "The lot of historical writers is hard; for if they tell the truth they provoke men, and if they write [what] is false they offend God."

## Truth Too Near the Heels

*Sir Walter Raleigh*: "Whosoever, in writing a modern history, shall follow truth too near the heels, it may haply strike out his teeth."

*Richard Hofstadter (Quoting Alain de Lille)*: "Authority has a nose of wax; it can be twisted in either direction."

## The National Offal

*On Sen. Joseph McCarthy*: That infernal doctor
draws out the miasma and dark exhalations
from the damp consciences of the Americans
who lived under boards. Kind responds to kind.
McCarthy is true to the America that doesn't
believe in freedom of thought, that lives meanly
and spitefully. In one sense he's a useful sewer
who floats away the national offal.

## Seizing the Good

*From Francis Parkman's Diary, 1846:* "The true philosophy of life is to seize with a ready and strong hand all the good in it, and to bear its inevitable evils as calmly and carelessly as may be."

## Love the Questions

*Rainer Maria Rilke*: "Be patient towards all that is unresolved in your heart. Try to love the questions themselves like . . . books that are written in a very foreign tongue."

## Incident in a Play

A young woman dresses in front of a mirror,
admiring herself, smiling in anticipation of the
approaching evening, and hums a tuneless song
in a husky sensual voice.

## A Note on William James

The great man "discovers" the community to itself. So Germany is Bismarcked into iron and won't become malleable. Great men ferment. They can twist and stimulate human proclivities. James, said Santayana, had the credulity of the true agnostic: anything half-baked is finally important. His father described Swedenborg as a reporter rather than a thinker, "though an egregiously intelligent one."

"Ruinous spring shall beat at our doors,
Root and shoot shall eat our eyes and our ears,
Disastrous summer burn up the beds of our
        streams
And the poor shall wait for another decaying
        October."

## Sequel to "The Man That Corrupted Hadleyburg"

Church leaders in Hadleyburg lament the decline of religion and the passion for money. What to do? A TV mogul advises them to sponsor a Bible Contest with a $65,000 prize to the winner. Everyone in the town begins to read the Bible. The town is reformed.

**Train Encounter**

In the Springfield train station. A tall, dark-complexioned, bleary-eyed man walks—or rather hobbles—by me and sits down. Homburg, dark-blue formfitting overcoat—slightly soiled and worn—dark-blue silk shirt with long pointed collar, no tie, cardboard suitcase, a cane, heavy brown leather gloves. Mustached. Cigar clamped in his mouth. Two-day growth of beard.

When he heard me mention Northampton to the conductor, he plunked himself beside me and opened up. The conversation continued until we arrived in Hamp. In an otherwise silent and decorous car filled with Smith and Amherst students and respectable folk, Lester Everett told "Danny" (as he quickly called me) that he'd been in the Vet's Hospital, that he'd paid $3.75 to get a taxi to South Station, that the "B" liner stopped at every fucking station and cow path, that he had the goods on Morin, that Alderman for Ward Two, that the Republican mayoral candidate had lived in Northampton for only three years and hadn't yet got the pulse of the city.

His epithets: "I'm telling you right to your kisser." "Danny, that Morin is a crock of shit. He hasn't got a pot to piss in or a window to throw it out of." "When I get to Northampton, I'm going to drop my valise at Young's Café, have a few drinks, have some more at Jim's and Monty's, and then run over to the Democratic headquarters. Mind you, I ain't got no animosity toward Morin. I'm a kind of philosophical guy. I always ask what's there in it for me." [From Cappy Lyons next day: Lester a chimney sweep (hence his sooty visage).]

## Neologisms

"Interlewd" (period of sensual desire);
"pencylmania" (passion for writing);
"symperise" (sympathize with exaggeration).

## From Monuments to Emoluments

*Sir Thomas Browne*: "Mummy is become merchandize. Mizraim cures wounds, and Pharaoh is sold for balsams."

## The Quintessence of Soul

*Hippolyte Taine on Alexander Pope*: "Once more,
let us come back to the truth, to that literary
truth which never forgets humanity, and com-
ports with a certain sympathy for all that deserve
it. If we can be just towards the ex-tinker Bunyan,
who in his fanatical visions shows force and
imagination, do not let us, on the other hand,
crush that charming witty creature, that quintessence of soul, that drop of keen wit wrapped
in cotton-wool, Pope. Let us not treat him
roughly, but as we take his hand to seat him in
our consulting, perhaps operating, chair let us do
nothing to make him cry out, were he yet living.
In literature, I should like always to proportion
our method to our subject, and to surround with
quite special precaution him who invites and
deserves him."

Taine speaks of "those writers who care only to
amuse, or to abandon themselves recklessly to
their antipathies."

## Illuminism

*Sir Herbert Read on Michelangelo and Bernini:*
Read notes his preference for austerity against
richness, a yearning for order and sobriety as
against a theatrical bravura. I can remember my
pleasure when I saw the Asamkirche in Munich.
Suddenly the Baroque seemed appropriate and
apt. Read suggests in his analysis of Bernini that
what I was responding to was "illuminism," the
use of sculpture to enhance a spurious response.
"To use art is to abuse art." He cites Adrian
Stokes—sculpture should appeal to our tactile
sensations as well as to our visual sensations and
be read "by the wordless Braille of undimmed
eyes."

## The Unseen Sweden

*W. B. Yeats*: "You have not seen Stockholm, everybody has said, until you have seen streets, houses, and trees all white with snow."

"The Scoundrel Patriot"

Into his final refuge crept
The Scoundrel Patriot and slept
Atop a catafalque of flags:
No one wept.

## Emerson Ever-Replenishing

*Isaac Rosenberg*: "That ebullition of the heart that seeks in novel but exact metaphor to express itself, the strong but delicate apocalyptical imagination that startles and suggests, the inward sanity that controls and directs—the mainspring of true poetry—is Emerson's."

Emerson considers a walk: "Plato thought 'exercise would almost cure a guilty conscience.' Sydney Smith said: 'You will never break down in a speech on a day when you have walked twelve miles.'"

Emerson says that health is the chief source of inspiration. And so are dreams "into whose farrago a divine lesson is sometimes slipped."

Emerson quotes Lorenzo Dow: "The Devil is the Lord's bulldog."

Emerson regarded the stars as the "tranquillizers of men." "In the fuss of the sunlight," he writes, "one might doubt [one's] identity."

RWE speaks of "having good luck" with a book.

John Milton a beloved model, cherished even

when criticized. Milton, says RWE, is enamored of beauty, finds truth the only source for genuine eloquence; is a patriot but much traveled, gifted in tongues, friend of illustrious men, chaste, abstemious—a morning-type rather than a nocturnal prowler, an experimenter of words, a Christian, an assumer of lowly duties—embodying (as no one else for Emerson) the Scholar's duties and opportunities, holding high converse with supernal powers while living and working with human clods. Considers no office mean. Devout, he attends no church. Lover and defender of political, religious, and domestic liberty.

I suppose what I find most rewarding in RWE, besides his tonic style, is his unceasing reminder that we are here *to live*. He writes to expectation and assures us of the marvels that any man can see every day. He also makes me yearn for wisdom, the undiminished bliss of the mind. Emerson is our Atlantic and Pacific, our Proteus, our ever-replenishing national dinner.

## The Body's Memory

*Plutarch*: "For do not think that old age is therefore evil spoken of and blamed because it is accompanied with wrinkles, gray hairs, and weakness of body; but this is the most trouble-some thing in old age, that it stains and corrupts the soul with remembrances of things relating to the body . . ."

*Pliny*: "When the young die, they have not had time to graft upon themselves the natural tangi-bilities—and pass more easily and less stubbornly into Spirit . . . Old age is not only more tolerable when recollections of physical bliss are dulled; it can become even desirable when conceived not as a stopping point but as the beginning of a more exciting pilgrimage."

## Epitaph for a Satirist

*W.H. Mallock*: "Two things only during his last years never palled upon him: one was, saying a sharp thing neatly; the other, detecting some new weakness in human nature. In this he seemed really to revel. On the littlenesses and pretenses of men, especially when they turned out failures, he seemed to look with a passionate contemptuous fondness, like a wicked prince on a peasant-girl."

## On Introspection

*C. S. Peirce*: "I would not advise a man to devote much time to observations on oneself. The great thing is to become emancipated from oneself . . . To make your own acquaintance does not mean Introspect your soul. It means see yourself as others would see you if they were intimate enough with you. Introspection, I mean a certain kind of fascinated introspection, on the contrary, is looking at yourself as nobody else will ever look at you, from a narrow, detached, and illusory point of view. Of course, a man must search his heart somewhat. It is highly needful. Only don't make a pursuit of it."

## On Writing & Invention

*T. E. Hulme*: "A man cannot write without seeing at the same time a visual signification before his eyes. It is this image which precedes the writing and makes it firm."

"The process of invention is that of gradually making solid the castles in the air." (Cp. H.D. Thoreau.)

"Fertility of invention" means remembrance of— accidental occurrences noted and arranged.

"Whitman had a theory that every object under the sun comes within the range of poetry. But he was too early in the day. It is no use having a theory that motor-cars are beautiful, and backing up this theory by working up an emotion not really felt. The object must cause the emotion before the poem can be written. Whitman's theory, that everything in America must be glorious, was his snare, because it was only a theory."

## On the Short Story

*Henry James:* "[T]he silver-shod, sober-paced, short-stepping, but oh so hugely nosing, so tenderly and yearningly and ruefully sniffing, grey mule of the 'few thousand words.'"

## On Forgiveness

*Pliny (the Younger):* "The highest character in my estimation is His, who is ready to pardon the moral errors of mankind as if he were every day guilty of some himself, and at the same time as cautious of committing a fault as if he never forgave one. It is a rule, then, which we upon all occasions, both private and public, most religiously observe, to be inexorable to our own feelings, while we treat those of the rest of the world with tenderness, not excepting even those who forgive none but themselves."

## On Dreams

*Bronson Alcott*: "Sleep and see; wake, and report the nocturnal spectacle. Sleep, like travel, enriches, refreshes by varying the day's perspective, showing us the night side of the globe we transverse day by day. We make transits too swift for our wakeful senses to follow; pass from solar to lunar consciousness in a twinkling, lapse from forehead and face to occupy our lower parts, and recover, as far as permitted, the keys of genesis and of the foreworlds."

*Bronson Alcott*: "Our dreams are characteristic of our working thoughts and states; we are never out of character; never quite another, even when fancy seeks to metamorphose us entirely."

*H. D. Thoreau*: "There is a moment in the dawn when the darkness of the night is dissipated, and before the exhalations of the day begin to rise, when we see all things more truly than at any other time . . . By afternoon, all objects are seen in mirage."

## Damnation

*John Selden*: "To preach long, loud, and damnation, is the way to be cried up. We love a man that damns us, and we run after him to save us."

**Daniel's Dictionary**

*Daysman*: (archaic) umpire, mediator. "Did he ask for any daysman between himself and God?"
—Elizabeth Peabody

## Preventing Rust

*Thoreau*: "We do not grow old. We rust old. Let us not consent to be old, but to die (live?) rather." One never grows old, Thoreau advises, if one keeps oneself burnished. "Rust." "Rust" might be likened to the incrustations that settle on body and soul after a person has withdrawn from nature and pursued low ends. God "has made us solitary agents." It is we who make our circumstances, but we can escape "rust" by concentrating on our "intra-stances."

## Sermonic Hells

*Jonathan Edwards*: "Sinners in the Hands of an Angry God." "The Future Punishment of the Wicked Unavoidable and Intolerable." "The Eternity of Hell Torments." "The Final Judgment." "The Wicked Useful in Their Destruction Only." "Wrath upon the Wicked to the Uttermost." "The End of the Wicked Contemplated by the Righteous."

*George Whitefield*: "The Eternity of Hell-Torments."

*John Wesley*: "The Great Assize." "The Signs of the Times." "Of Hell."

Topics to investigate: "The Sociology of Hell." "Comparative Hells." "Roman Catholic and Protestant Hell Compared."

"The possibilities of delight were worth the eventualities of torture ... Oh, I am caught in the 'man-forg'd manacles,' though in this case they are not the manacles of reason, but the manacles of a relentless, unreasoning memory."

"If decisions were a choice between alternatives, decisions would come easy. Decision is in the selection and formulation of alternatives."

"God pity the man or nation wise in proverbs ... for there is much error gone into the collecting of such a store."

We should all be peripatetics, thinking while we walk (cp. Thoreau). "Sedentary" is a bad word for Burke. It implies the fixed, the planted, the mechanical. The artist should strive to do more than to set down his ideas on paper. He must also live his art and express himself "in vital social relationships."

## Story Idea: Bluebeard

He doesn't decapitate his "wives." He woos them, collects their photographs, which he keeps in a drawer. The poor women suffocate and Bluebeard weeps—but more for himself than for his victims.

## The Mosquito's Dogma

*John Adams to His Son, Nov. 13, 1816:* "Let the
Human mind loose. It must be loose. It will be
loose. Superstition and despotism cannot confine
it. And the conclusion must be that Musquitos
are not competent to dogmatize."

## On the Letters and Memoirs of Charles Kingsley

*Henry James*: "When towards the close of such a career, the sympathetic reader finds Mr. Kingsley installed as Professor of History at Cambridge, or engaged in theological controversy with Dr. Newman, he feels as if in offering him these remarkable opportunities for making an unfavorable appearance, fate were playing him a trick which he had not done enough to deserve . . . He saw admirably, though he thought confusedly."

HJ quotes from a letter CK wrote to a friend: "Do not reject Wardlow because he is a Presbyterian. The poor man was born so, you know. It is very different from a man's dissenting personally."

(Note HJ's interest in Chartism and British working class: possible connection with *The Princess Casamassima?*)

## Daniel's *Pomes*

"Wordsworth Misremembered"

Good God! I'd rather suckle pagans
In my worn-out tweeds.

## Note to Future Self

*Nov.* 20: For future reference—very bad times.
Crisis piled on crisis.

*July 29*: Met Stuart Hughes at bus stop in
Northampton. After a sandwich lunch, we took
off for Talcottville some 180 miles away. Much
talk going and returning. During the two days
in Boone County, each of us revealed private
thoughts without restraint.

Wilson had just stepped out of his bathtub when
we arrived. He dressed, came downstairs, and
proceeded to flout his alcohol-free regimen.
We dined in Constableville and retired early.

EW tired and flushed, now looks like his grand-
father whose daguerreotype hangs over the
fireplace. I note EW's rigid mouth, the corners
turning downward, the dewlaps. Light comes
into his eyes and expression returns to his face
when he is moved or excited or amused, but it
passes away as quickly as it appears. Now he
scents death the way he scents a good story. He's
weighed down. Much affected by Hemingway's
death, I think, and a little afraid, and is preparing
his extensive notebooks for publication.

Fiction doesn't interest him much at this stage.
History does, but I suspect that the Civil War
book that has preoccupied him for so many
years will soon be behind him. He asked Stuart

and me to read the introduction. We did—but neither of us liked it. We advised him to publish it separately, that it seemed to us a personal harangue that had little to do with the substance of his book. Not so, declared Edmund. When you've read it, you'll see that the introduction is necessary.

During our walk to the underground river, he spoke about his undergraduate days, his reading (George Borrow, Flaubert, Huysmans, Shaw, Arnold Bennett, Wells), his trick chair that would collapse into a pair of scissors when sat on (the old sadist reflected in the young). He spoke of his hospital experiences in World War I and sang a verse of "Lydia Pinkham" I'd never heard:

> Now Elsie Jones—had no breastworks,
> Couldn't even fill her blouse,
> But she took, she took the Vegetable Compound.
> Now they milk her with the cows.

Sunday morning found EW wandering around, almost drunk. Said he'd been naughty and drank alone until the sun came up. Then he went to bed and slept until almost noon. I think he will be sorry to see us leave—and glad, too.

"The Scholar"

So soaked was he in books, so learning fraught,
It almost might be said his body thought.

## Richard Hofstadter's Head and Heart

Starting draft of Dick's book on anti-intellectualism in America. The war between Head and
Heart (he doesn't put it that way) is waged at
all times and places, but Dick believes that it
flourished in the untrammeled terrain of Virgin
America. Certainly, the "Enthusiasts" will be
critically judged, but I wonder how he would
respond to the following comments: (1) Emerson
and Whitman were right. The old systole of head
and heart is mutually necessary. (2) The Good
Society is never attainable: it keeps shifting from
bad to worse to better. (3) When the engines
of the social power plant are torpid, more air
(enthusiasm, spirit) is required. When the fires
flare up too hotly and brightly, the airflow is
reduced. The antinomian can be a curse—but on
occasion a blessing.

## Death from Above

*Spinoza*: "It is not good to fear death, nor right to long for death. The scales must be so balanced that the pointer is vertical."

## Transcendental Man

*Samuel Daniel*: "Unless above himself he can /
Erect himself, how poor a thing is man."

## Vita/Mors

*Si vis vitam, para mortem.* "If you want to endure life, prepare yourself for death." Or we might add—if you want to enjoy or savor life, prepare for death.

## Vastation

A key term in the Swedenborgian Dictionary and well known to the students of Henry James, whose father and brother William (and possibly HJ himself) suffered "vastations."

What does it mean? Swedenborg defines it as a "deviation," a "declension," a falling away from grace, a turn toward the direction of hell. A person experiencing a vastation is "descending from heaven, but not yet arrived at hell." For long periods he occupies a boundary-less limbo, deviating or declining from a grace he never achieved or perhaps even suspected. Swedenborg likens a man whose rational principles are solely derived through the senses (and not by heavenly affection) to a goose or a parrot, for that is how his voice sounds to angels.

Note: "Parrots and Geese" are synonyms for Bouvards and Pécuchets, Babbitts, Philistines, Men of Understanding, Squares, etc. And note the many emblematic birds in the Swedenborgian Correspondence chart: Partridge, Pelican, Hawk, Eagle, Owl.

## Homage to the Pulps

Title for my unwritten reflection on F. L. Packard,
Sax Rohmer, Edgar Rice Burroughs, Achmed
Abdullah, Zane Grey.

## Volunteer

A word introduced to me by Eudora Welty. Defined by the dictionary as "springing up spon-
taneously" or "without being planted." In my
fancies, Volunteers are children in God's garden,
heavenly bastards who simply and beautifully
appeared. *Volunteer* a signifier for the delightfully
unwanted, a gentle name for the brave illegitimate child.

## The Chill of Idealism

*Emerson:* "Don't be so tender at making an enemy
now and then. Be willing to go to Coventry
sometimes, and let the populace bestow on you
their coldest contempts. The finished man of the
world must eat of every apple once. He must hold
his hatreds also at arm's length, and not remember spite. He has neither friends nor enemies,
but values men only as channels of power."
(The last sentence might be J. F. Kennedy's
epitaph and the whole passage in keeping with
Melville's animadversions in *The Confidence-Man*.
Did Emerson ever see his friends and contemporaries as any more than emblems? His idealism
can chill. I think this is what Melville feared and
wondered at.)

Emerson had no tolerance for sickness, although
he had suffered physical ailments. "Nervous
problems," an editor notes, "he could hardly
understand or pardon," and he quoted approv-
ingly Samuel Johnson's remark that "Every man
is a rascal as soon as he is sick ... For sickness is
a cannibal which eats up all the life and youth
it can lay hold of and absorbs its own sons and
daughters. I figure it as a pale, wailing, distracted
phantasy absolutely selfish, heedless of what is
good and great, attentive to its sensations, losing

its soul, and afflicting other souls with meanness and mopings and with ministration to its voracity of trifles."

Emerson on the futility of travel. Its only valid purpose is to discover one's country. "One day we shall cast out the passion for Europe by the passion for America."

Emerson on blockheads and their power to benumb. Nonsense can refresh, but "a virulent aggressive fool taints the reason of a household." "A fly is as untamable as a hyena."

Robert Musil's novel begins in Vienna, 1913, but
the day and the place less important than the
time. It could just as well be Paris or London or
Rome—if not New York. Musil notes the power,
human and mechanical, generated in this interval
of well-being, but it is directionless and running
over and above and below century-old institutions unequipped to cope with the dislocations
that block and divert the riverbeds of progress.
By 1913, silt and rocks have piled up and soon
the roar of angry waters raging over unbolstered
banks will terrify the world. Henry James had his
premonitions, and so did Joyce and some of the
Marxist intelligentsia and a few social scientists.
In America, younger and seemingly beyond the
threat of flood, there were few such premonitions. Take a year—say 1913 or 1919—and look at it
from the point of view of a literary seismologist.
What were writers, scholars, artists writing and
thinking and doing in those years? Were they
as befuddled and uncomprehending as the rest?
Were they the "antennae" of the race?

Musil on the Realist and the Possibilist (we might
call him the "Emersonian" or "Thoreauvian" man)
who sees reality as ductile and fluid. The man of
possibility, says Musil, assumes that a thing might

just as well be something else. He has a "creative disposition." Such people "not infrequently make the things other people admire appear wrong and the things that other people prohibit permissible, or even make both appear a matter of indifference. Such possibilitarians live, it is said, within a finer web, a web of haze, fantasy and the subjunctive mood. In their presence such people are referred to as crackbrains, dreamers, weaklings, know-alls, and carpers and cavillers."

"Possibilitarians" are not deficient in a sense of reality. They simply don't stop where most people do. Their role is to awaken their fellows who keep doing the same thing over and over again. The possibilitarian may act strangely. He will "always be unreliable and incalculable in his intercourse with other people," but he will be satisfied "about everything as soon as it can be summed up in an extraordinary idea." He is an idealist.

## Texas Is Our Congo

*JFK's Assassination (Nov. 22)*: A few hours ago,
as I was sitting in my office typing a recommen-
dation, Ruiz came in to tell me that the President
had been assassinated. The reports were not
definite; he was still alive when taken to the hospital, but his condition was said to be critical, as
was Governor Connally's. Over at the coffee shop,
we learned more blurred details, and then the
announcement came that the President was dead.
Everyone expresses the same feeling of stunned
disbelief. In an academic place like Smith, the
next response is anger against the barbaric mur-
derers and the Southern milieu in which they are
permitted to flourish. Where was the FBI, so hot
for the Communist adolescents going to Cuba,
so eager to hound any alleged Communists, so
lukewarm or actually sympathetic to the anti-
Negro rioters and those who would impeach
Justice Warren? Who can even begin to anticipate the consequences of these rifle shots
reverberating around the world? Now the Vice
President is acting head of the country. What
about next year? Will he represent the Democratic Party? Will the President's brother? And
does this assure the election of Nixon? Will
Goldwater dare to run, after his friendly gestures to the Birchites? And without a firm hand

directing our foreign policy, what is the outcome for the millions outside the United States?

*Sunday*: The bizarre events continue—the assassin assassinated. Texas is our Congo, and the city of Dallas pulsates with hatred. No one can quite believe that the killings occurred, and yet each new morning deepens the magnitude of the national turmoil.

## Unfit for Beards

*Alice Meynell's "Laughter"*: ". . . the Oriental estimate of laughter as a thing fitter for women, fittest for children, and unfitted for the beard."

## Idea for Play: Whitman's Masks

All characters are masks of the protagonist:
Mr. Walter Whitman, Walt (the Christ carpenter), the private Walt Whitman, the Prophet,
the Good Gray Poet.

*Plot*: The Poet emerges—first the brash editori-
alist. The period of incubation followed by the
Carpenter persona. Then the private anguish
of the unrequited lover. Next the elegist of the
Civil War, and last, the "Bard."

*Title*: "One Man's Performance, *A Life of Walt
Whitman Self-told*, in five sections taken from
his poems, letters, journals, reported words."

## The Rotten Bucolic

*Nathanael West's Wasteland*: (1) Love vs. hate: the
drying up of promise mocked and ridiculed, and
self-laceration with West, the wounded comic,
mocking & railing and jeering at what he yearns
for. West's "west" (California, Hollywood) is the
land of the cheated. Nothing left but frustration,
unfulfillment & hate. In *The Day of the Locust*,
the wasteland of the Birch society is unfructified
by Goldwaterish rains. (2) A study of infernal
millenarianism. The people have moved "West"
to the last Eden and are now enacting the final
chapter of a blasted dream. Notice West's paro-
dies of the Edenic myth in *Miss Lonelyhearts*, and
in the make-believe movie sets of Hollywood,
the pasteboard masks concealing the decayed
reality. (3) Bucolic America gone rotten in *A Cool
Million*.

## Robert Musil

*On Philosophers*: "Philosophers are violent and aggressive persons who, having no army at their disposal, bring the world into subjection to themselves by means of locking it up in a system. Probably that is also the reason why there have been great philosophic minds in times of tyranny, whereas times of advanced civilization and democracy do not succeed in producing a convincing philosophy, at least so far as one can judge from the lamentations one commonly hears on the subject."

*On Essays and Essayists*: "The translation of the word 'essay' as 'attempt,' which is the generally accepted one, only approximately gives the most important allusion to the literary model. For an essay is not the provisional or incidental expression of a conviction that might on a more favorable occasion be elevated to the status of truth or that might just as easily be recognized as error . . . an essay is the unique and unalterable form that a man's inner life assumes in a decisive thought. Nothing is more alien to it than that irresponsibility and semi-finishedness of mental images known as subjectivity . . . There have been quite a number of such essayists and masters of the floating life within . . . Their domain lies between religion and knowledge, between example and doctrine, between *amor intellectualis* and poetry, they are saints with and without religion, and sometimes too they are simply men who have gone out on an adventure and lost their way."

The wisdom of essayists can't be extracted and practiced, can't be transformed into a "theory of life." "What is left over is about as much as remains of a jelly-fish's delicately opalescent body after it has been lifted out of the water and laid on the sand. The teachings of the inspired crumble into dust in the rationality of the unin-spired, crumble into contradiction and nonsense."

*On Mind and Body*: "And, oddly enough, the majority of people have either a neglected body, formed and deformed by accidental circum-stances and seemingly in almost no relationship to their mind and character, or one hidden under the mask of sport, which gives it the look of those hours when it takes time off from being itself. For those are the hours when man continues the day-dream of wanting to look like something, which he has casually picked up from the illustrated papers of the smart, great world. All these bronzed and muscular tennis-players, horsemen and motorists, who all have a record-breaking look, although usually they are only moderately good at whatever it is they do, these ladies in full dress or undress, are day-dreamers, only distinguished from ordinary waking dreamers by the fact that their dreams do not remain inside the brain, but, issuing forth *en masse* into the open air, take shape as a formation of the mass-soul, physically, dramatically, and (one feels inclined to say, thinking of certain more than dubious occult phenomena), ideoplastically."

### Daniel's Dictionary

*Myrmecophile*: (Gk. *Myrmex*) any insect (a beetle, say) that settles in an ant colony, or a Westerner in the USSR.

## Some Aphorisms

*Hugo von Hofmannsthal*: "While growing older we recognize that throughout all the vicissitudes of life we are not free of guilt; but in each of us there dwells our own form of innocence, which is what sustains us without our knowing how."

"Circumstances have less power than we think to make us unhappy; but the anticipation of future circumstances has a gigantic one."

"The meaning of marriage is natural dissolution and palingenesis. Thus true marriage dissolves only in death—indeed, not even then."

"Joy requires more surrender, more courage, than pain. As far as we surrender to joy, we challenge the unknown darkness."

## Mere Intellect?

In coming years, historians of American history will have much to say about the "consensus" school of the 1950s and 1960s. The "consensus" historians have tended to play down the disharmonies and clashes featured by progressive and Marxist historians in post-WWII America and have signaled triumphs as much as or more than failures. It is sometimes said that these "celebrations" are the work of historians who "never had it so good," who are allegedly part of the new Establishment.

More interesting to me, however, are the explorations made during the past years into the American popular mind—the new looks at populism, education, and religion—what Dick Hofstadter included in the term "anti-intellectualism." That many movements, men, institutions hitherto canonized by liberals and radicals were at bottom distrustful of *mere intellect* is easily borne out. Nowhere can the historian find better examples than in the years between 1800 and 1860.

Now, in the light of our own experiences, we read again the arguments of the Federalist elite and "anti-mobocratic" Whigs against democratic ferment; and we do so with a new sympathy, because the warnings of the pessimists have not by any means proved to be illusory. The millennial faith of the evangelized pragmatic, utilitarian Jacksonianism seems childish and tragically inadequate in 1963. Less apparent to many is the failure of the Conservatives to provide an adequate social program. Each age seems to get what it needs and perhaps deserves.

## "Safe" Neighborhoods

Frank Ellis told me about an advertisement
for new homes in Kansas City—"Exclusive in a
friendly way," not rudely exclusive, mind you,
but assuring the purchaser that his new property
will be "safe." Safe from what? Safe from Negro
neighbors. At a time when the world is highly
unsafe, advertisers trivialize the word. Deodorants will keep us "safe" for 24 hours from "offend-
ing." Americans should not be exclusive but
neither should they "offend." A Springfield jewelry store advertises "Peace of mind guaranteed."

## The Deist's Assent

"From the close of General Washington's administration in 1797, to the inauguration of General Harrison, there was not more than one message to Congress, or inaugural address, in which the Christian religion was distinctly recognized. Most [of] the annual messages during that period . . . expressed little or nothing to which a Deist might not assent." (See John Bodo, *The Protestant Clergy and Public Issues* [1954].) Note: James Madison especially critical of those who would introduce religious denominationalism into public business.

## Symbology of Money?

*Musil on Rich Men*: A subject more often described than analyzed ... What is the rich man like? What moves him? Are the rich another race, as Fitzgerald insisted? Not enough to narrate (gloatingly, angrily, wonderingly) anecdotes of their display. Musil is one of the few who writes of the rich man with real understanding.

(1) Rich man likely to insist that money has nothing to do with value of a person. (2) Implication: that he would be as valuable and important without his wealth. (3) Intelligentsia often fail to realize this. They usually have no money, but they have a high esteem for themselves and don't feel diminished by their want of it. (4) They ask the rich man for money, not seeing that this same rich man would prefer to assist them with his ideas. (5) For him, to give money away puts the giver "into a position antagonistic to the nature of money," which should be preserved, tended, guarded, and dispensed only for the purpose of bringing in greater returns, literal or psychic. Thus lavish expenditures, public or personal, are not antagonistic to the money spirit, but quiet and unnoticed giving "can only be compared to foully murdering one's money." (6) Rich people are often socialists. They object to being told that

their money comes to them as a result of certain social laws. They are quite willing to talk about a future when no property exists. The rich give but always modestly. Prefer to give to people who attribute their generosity not so much to their large supplies of money but to their intelligence.

Query: Why not an anthology, "The Symbology of Money"?

Reading life of Poe by Wagenknecht, a storehouse of lore, biographical and critical. What emerges thus far is the child-man who exhibits very early the shrill precocity of the gifted child but who never "matures" into adulthood. Another way to put it (and this is W's line) would be to say that Poe never capitulated, sold out, compromised, came to terms with the world: so we see him, perhaps, as a symbol of the child-self who didn't grow hard—who arouses sympathy, concern, and guilt.

I notice, too, that Poe, deeply affected by pathos, wept at the death of Little Nell. When he came to the pathetic parts of his works, his eyes would be suffused in tears, and he couldn't go on. The farther we can remove ourselves from the proximity of death, the easier it is to be tough and impersonal. Now the dead are whisked away. In the Victorian era, the ceremonies and the paraphernalia of crying were much more in evidence. The moribund man was not hidden away in hospitals. He lay among his relics and heard the music of mortality.

*Abhor*: to protest against, or reject formally—a term of canon law. (We have lost that connection, but I think we should retain it.) "Abhor" means more than revulsion. It is more positive, active, stronger. "Sir, I abhor your principles!"

*Abject*: a base, despicable person. "You abject!" (No pity here.)

*Acersecomick*: one whose hair was never cut.

*Addle-plot*: a person who spoils any amusement.

*Agonious*: full of agony.

*Air-dew*: an old name for manna.

*All-manner-a-wat*: indiscriminate abuse.

*Almond-for-a-parrot*: some trifle to amuse a silly person.

*Anfractuosities*: mazy and involved turnings and windings.

*Anshum-scranchum*: process that goes on when too many people are scrambling for an insufficient amount of food.

*Bag*: to breed or become pregnant. "Venus shortly bagged, and ere long was Cupid bred."

*Ballocke-stones*: testicles; in 1540, a term of endearment as well.

*Barn-mouse*: a bat.

*Barnacles*: popular name for spectacles.

*Purting-glumpot*: a sullen fellow.

## So Far Out, You're In

*On Paul Goodman*: Let's imagine him the hero of a 1960s picaresque novel in which academia, New York City, and Washington provide the backdrop. His career begins as a student at the City College of New York, and he moves up the scale via Columbia. He is bright, urban if not urbane, and his dream of a quasi-rural community—relaxed, beautiful, sexually free—combines the idealized attributes of an anarchist boardinghouse and Garden City. But the mainline of this parable follows his stint at a Black Mountain type of school, his writing on psychiatry, his poetry, and his "frank" novels. How does he succeed? Perhaps by publishing an esoteric-erotic book reviewed in avant-garde magazines that are closely watched by Time-Life Inc. as symptomatic of the "New." He reaches the point where he is so far *Out* that he becomes *In*. Then the invitations pour in. He gets on the college foundation circuit, goes to Washington, etc., etc.

## Daniel's Dictionary

*Bedaffe*: to make a fool of.

*Bedpresser*: dull heavy fellow.

*Begrumpled*: displeased.

*Bellycheer*: good living.

*Bladge*: a low woman.

*Break-danse*: a treacherous person.

*Bubble-and-Squeak*: a dish composed of beef and cabbage.

*Zwodder*: a drowsy and stupid state of body and mind.

L. P. Smith suggests adoption of English equivalents for Latinate words: *Make-sleepy* (soporific), *moody-headed* (melancholy), *dish-down* (disappointment), *day-lived* (ephemeral).

## God, The Electric Torch

*Musil*: "If something is to be valid and have a name, it must be repeatable, many specimens of it must exist—if you had never seen the moon before, you would think it was an electric torch. Incidentally, the great embarrassment God causes to science consists in Him having been only once, and that at the creation of the world before there were any trained observers on the spot."

"He ran his mind swiftly over what separated him from this new generation. These young people contradicted each other in all and everything; the only things they had definitely in common was the attack on objectivity, intellectual responsibility, and the balanced personality."

## Poetry's Secretions

A. E. Housman wrote to Al Fisher in 1925:
"A poem is a secretion like pearls or Indian
rubber; it needs cleaning and trimming, which
is an art, and all art is based upon some science."

## Greetings from Belfast?

"Can you stick it?" (How are you?).
"Aye" (tough Calvinism).

## Greetings from Hell

"Danny, we're put on earth to suffer."
(Daily greeting of Frank Kretzschmer,
a Smith College janitor.)

**Book Title**

*The Anonymous Company: The Happily
Undistinguished and Their Work.*

## Friday's Fare

In "Enoch Arden," Walter Bagehot noted,
Tennyson spoke of the village "whose Friday
fare was Enoch's ministering," meaning that
Enoch sold fish to the village.

## Note for Our Times

*March* 5: News item: The police officer hand-cuffed to Oswald when Oswald was shot by Ruby declared today that he had been blinded by the lights from the TV cameras when he emerged with his prisoner. Therefore he could not see Ruby approaching Oswald with a drawn gun. (The light that obscures; the pitiless light of publicity. What a comment on our news agencies.)

## Thought for the Week: Eggs

*William Jennings Bryan*: "The egg is the most universal of foods and its uses date from the beginning, but what is more mysterious than an egg? . . . We eat eggs, but we cannot explain an egg."

## Daniel's Dictionary

*Locuplete*: (rare) wealthy. In a letter, Emerson referred to his brother Charles as a "pleasing stripling, & locuplete of friends."

*Coacervate*: (rare) to heap, to pile up; gathering or accumulation. Emerson to Theodore Parker: What "a marked growth in power, & *coacervation*, shall I say."

*Malison*: (archaic or dial.) a curse. "I call no shadowy malison / Upon thy fair young brow." —J. G. Whittier

*Hunks*: a crabbed disagreeable person. A covetous sordid miser. "Now Bildad, I am sorry to say, had the reputation of being an incorrigible old hunks." —*Moby Dick*

*Snudge*: a miser, a mean or sneaking fellow. "Thus your husbandrye, methincke, is more like life of a covetous snudge, that ofte very evill proves, then the labour of a good husbande, that knoweth well what he doth." —Roger Ascham, *Toxophilus*

*Euhemerism*: from Euhemerus, who held that polytheistic mythology arose from the deification of dead heroes—hence derivation of mythology from history.

## Hammers and Anvils

*Butler's* Lives of the Saints, *III*, 262: "It was a saying St. Dominic frequently repeated, that a man
who governs his passions is master of the world.
We must either rule them or be ruled by them.
It is better to be the hammer than the anvil."
(Note: Melville, in *Benito Cereno*, changes the
name of *The Tryall* to the *St. Dominick*.) Cereno
is the anvil; Babo is the hammer.

## Desecrations

Walden Pond, the Eye of Nature, the Circle
comprehending the inexpressible. Thoreau the
surly seer who turns Walden into Diogenes' tub.
The cant of Thoreau by people who obliterate his
vision. We praise him and desecrate his counsels—
as we do God's. The encroachment of filth, the
anti-Nature crusade, the obliteration of privacy,
the tumor-state, the cant of war and the murder-
ous implementation.

## Notes from All Over

Self-Realization Fellowship (Los Angeles)

The Thinking Car's Gasoline

Tooth, Line, and Sinker

Sat on or swallowed his own Petard

Elizabeth Taylor's mother

Psycho-semitic illness

## Barry, Barry, We Want Barry!

*Goldwater and the Goldwaterites, July 15:* A hot
muggy day. A big crane is knocking the Students
Building to pieces. A hot-waterish convention
in S. F. electing Barry Goldwater, the darling of
the Birchers and the organized Know-Nothings
who have seized the Republican Party. Perhaps
a new era in this country, not in 1964 (when
Goldwater partisans will be smashed) but in
the coming years. The small pursy, mean-faced
people screaming "Barry, Barry, we want Barry"
and the sullen clean-cut corps of youth raised
in the towns of the middle west, southwest,
southern California, are part of the new middle
class frightened by the ugly signs of urbanism,
delinquency, Big Government. The New Wealth
financing the show is bucking the Older Wealth.
These people are anti-East, anti-literary, anti–
Wall Street, anti-Negro, anti-Jew. What for is
hard to say: perhaps better homes, gardens, better
swimming pools, cook-outs, ranch-type houses,
motorboats, and football. Barry is their Hitler.
Eisenhower (whose perceptible deliquescence is
perhaps the saddest part of the spectacle) their
Hindenburg. The Goldwaterites are organized,
passionate, religious—"cynical innocents." They
have no sense of Europe, little fear of war.
Henry Adams would have understood them and

shuddered. Henry Cabot Lodge appreciates the threat of their imbecility. He calls them "that crowd."

## Jumping Out of Our Skins

*Oct. 16*: Fateful day. British Labour wins; Khrushchev out; Chinese explode bomb; scandal over Jenkins incident, and possible embarrassment to the President at this most delicate time. History comes in bunches. No matter how long anticipated, it explodes and millions jump out of their skins. There are times when men seem to take over and shape their destinies, and times when events simply get out of hand and "ride mankind."

## Story Idea: About a Women's College

*Opening Sentence*: "Looking down upon the rows of young women as they gazed expectantly up at him, he saw them as 'a chain of redoubts and breastworks raised by besiegers about the place invested'—contravallations which he was about to storm."

## Resolved

"To beseech no man for his helping and to vex no god with prayer."—William Morris, *The Story of Sigurd the Volsung and the Fall of the Niblungs*

## Reversing Clichés

"The razor was as sharp as the mind of a very intelligent man." "The coral was ruby-lipped." "The pearls were as white as a set of teeth that had been thoroughly cleaned." "The young girl's cheek was as soft as a damask napkin."

## On the Absurd

*Santayana*: "I agree that a perpetual search for
the incongruous, even if it keeps us laughing
mechanically, is empty and vulgar and disgusting
in the end. It is a perpetual punning in images.
And yet I feel that there is a genuine spirit of
humour abroad in America, and that it is one of
the best things there. The constant sense of the
incongruous, even if artificially stimulated and
found only in trivial things, is an admission that
existence is absurd; it is therefore a liberation of
the spirit . . . because the spirit is glad to be free;
and yet it is not a scornful nor bitter liberation,
because a world that lets us laugh at it and be
free is after all a friendly world. We have no need
to bear that serious grudge against it which we
should be justified in bearing if it fooled us altogether, and tortured us by its absurdities instead
of amusing us and making us spiritually free."

## Cretan Saying

"Return where you have failed, leave where you have succeeded."

### In the Dentist's Chair

Endlessly amused by my unspoken wit,
I dream up molar comedies of pain
Where Thief is Time and Time is toothlessness.

Ruthlessly the Robbing Robber robs
Six white sepulchers befouled with stain—
First blasts, then excavates the charnel pit.

Unperturbed by rolling eyes or sobs,
He thrills the drill; he numbs the ear with roar.
Plunge steel! I choke on gobs of bloody spit.

After such agitation, all is ache,
Reverberating throb, expanding sore:
Under the tartar plain lies truth of tooth.

Introduction to the Dickensian world grand and
mysterious, a series of Chinese boxes built into
each other, vast, deep, humming with coincidence. Beyond the dark and storm-swept, a
providential force, England is a great box filled
with smaller boxes, and London is a prison inside
a prison, and Dombey's house is a prison in a
prison in a prison. All is determined and charted
like the streets, but the streets aren't arranged
like a grid; they turn and dip and disappear
and re-emerge. These narrow avenues are the
arteries. Characters are types & archetypes.
Here is Benevolence and Greed and Simpering
Foolishness. Each is an abstraction of a thousand
particulars, animated by the energy of their cre-
ator and roused into movement and speech. He
pushes them onto a stage where they speak and
posture before exiting. But such is their vitality
and vividness that they persist after they depart
and continue as epiphenomena. What is real and
most alive in his books are things—the clothes
and furniture and houses. A fairy tale: Dombey is
a blasted emperor in thrall to a dark power. This
is a novel about a long imprisonment and final
illumination.

## Names

"Fan Staunton," "Hope Mariner."

## Bedeviled Eggs

William Morris shouts to his cook, "Mary! Those eggs are bad! I'll eat them, but don't let it happen again."

## The Good Jobbers

*Quote from Carlyle's Diary*: "On leaving the house today, I noticed that the men at the corner were more than usually drunk. And then I remembered that it was the birthday of their Redeemer."

*Ford Madox Hueffer (Ford)*: "To make a good job of a given task is the highest thing in life."

## Ladies!

An Englishman comments on the American
habit of referring to all women as "ladies."
The quintessence of this usage in an alleged
passage in a Methodist sermon: "Who were the
last at the Cross? Ladies! Who were earliest at
the grave? Ladies!"

## On the Creative Process

The germ of Goethe's *Werther* came simultaneously with news of a friend's suicide: "[A]t that instant the plan of *Werther* was found, the whole shot together from all directions, and became a solid mass, as the water in a vase, which just at the freezing point, is changed by the slightest concussion into ice . . . The main work is done; the rest is merely setting it down—the task of an artisan rather than an artist."

## Goethe's Greek

*Bayard Taylor Quoting Goethe*: "Let each one be a Grecian, in his own way: but let him *be* one!"

## Transmissions from Gods and Devils

Norman Mailer's *The Presidential Papers* is
more interesting than *An American Dream* and
certainly more real. NM is a Manichean, a comic
Nietzsche, Charlie Chaplin. He wants to live his
thoughts. God and the Devil speak to him, and
he transmits their messages in the metaphors of
violence, scatology, and the absurd.

## Writers and Politics

*Conor Cruise O'Brien*: "The more nearly mono-
lithic the lie-structure of competing power-blocs,
the less the possibility of communication between them, and the greater fear which they
inspire in one another . . . Peaceful coexistence,
which requires some degree of mutual confidence, demands *ipso facto* a reduction in the
lie-content of human exchange."

"All weak people are apt to cherish a sense of
superior virtue, corresponding to the magnitude of the crimes they have been powerless
to commit."

"To be able to entertain (to receive with mental
courtesy, civility) the most abhorrent ideas and
before rejecting them, hold them—as it were—
in suspension, scrutinizing them, examining the
revulsion they provoke and assessing the possible
reasons for this revulsion."

"Above all—there should never be a spiritual
or mental 'No Admittance' sign to the ideas or
propositions, plans or programs, assumptions
and value judgments that are (at the moment)
excluded from our thought-systems. I mean, we
must be careful, in our zeal for private or public

truths, not to exalt the beleaguered mind with its parapets and sentries. Our metaphors should be the inn on the country road, accepting any wayfaring idea that can pay its way, not welcoming it indiscriminately but not summarily telling it to get along. This is not sentimental open-mindedness that declines to exert any standards to judgment."

## "Anecdotes of Mr. Keuner"

*Brecht's* Tales from the Calendar: Mr. K said,
"The thinking man does not use too much light,
not too much bread, nor an idea too many."

Mr. K's answer when someone asks him if there
is a God: "I'd advise you to reflect whether,
depending upon the answer to this question,
your behavior would alter. If it would not, we can
drop the question. If it would, then at least I can
be of some help to you by telling you that your
mind is already made up: you need a God."

When Mr. K heard that he had been praised by
his former pupils, he said: "Long after the pupils
have forgotten the master's failings, he himself
remembers them."

"'What are you working on?' Mr. K was asked.
'I'm having a lot of trouble: I'm preparing my
next mistake,' answered Mr. K."

"A man who had not seen Mr. K for a long
time greeted him with the words, 'You haven't
changed at all!' 'Oh!' said Mr. K and turned pale."

**From Sarah Taylor Shatford,** *Birds of Passage*

A young girl dreaming of last night's joy,
When her hand was won by a handsome boy,
Gazes with loving and steady glare
On a beautiful diamond solitaire.

## Paul Valéry

PV admired the Roman Catholic church but likened it to a school whose best students are expelled. He is an anarchist/conformist: his hatred of disorder. Skeptical, courteous, tolerant— but when young an anti-Dreyfusard.

*To Gide, 1918*: "Last night, re-read *Das Kapital* . . . I am one of the few who have read it. The big book has remarkable things in it . . . at times a desert of pedantry; but some of its analyses are marvelous. I mean that method of getting at things is like the one I sometimes use, and I can frequently translate his language into mine."

*On Anarchy*: "Anarchy is the individual's effort to refuse obedience to any injunction the basis of which cannot be verified."

*On Myths (of Politics)*: To murder, kill, be killed, tortured for something you neither know nor care about.

*On People*: Substitute for it "number" and "mixture" and then test higher-sounding slogan "the sovereign mixture," the "will of the mixture."

*On the Left*: "The heart of the weak is hideous; anyone who suffered for a just cause or a creed has a poisonous serpent in his heart."

*On the Center*: "The middle groups are those who fear and hate to the right and left of them."

*On the Right*: "The rightists have never had brains enough to pretend they have a heart."

*On All Parties*: "Hatred, cruelty, hypocrisy, and graft belong to no single party, stupidity to no single regime, error to no single system."

*In Sum*: One might say that for Valéry, the literary is always thought long processed. Note how he resists the subconscious and the inspirational. He's suspicious of the "too immediate." Such "immediate" thoughts may be spoken but not written. Always the intellect—never the institutions. Goal: intellectual power, detachment, the exhaustion of the irrelevant—but never for glory: "And as for glory, no. To shine in one another's eyes is to get for them the glitter of false jewelry."

## On Style

*Paul Valéry:* "Every fine style has been acquired in circles or coteries, and all excellent language comes from a pose or affectation, from competition and selection, as the result of refined pride, the aristocratic sense, disdain for the rank and file, and a secret tendency not to be understood by everybody—to create for oneself a difficult mode of speech—a password—a jargon. Classical language is very noble slang." (I think Henry James would have said "Amen" to this passage.)

**Faith in Moods**

*Emerson's Consolatory Note to Carlyle after Jane Carlyle's "Gentle Departure"*: "We would not for ourselves count covetously the descending steps, after we have passed the top of the mount, or grudge to spare some of the days of decay."

*Carlyle Replies, Jan. 27, 1867*: A wry and angry and poignant letter, his own misery foremost though he has tender comments about the departed wife. Speaks of the 12 years' agony writing his *Frederick* (note: for Carlyle, a book is always a vengeful opponent to be overcome, after which the exhausted author pants in weakness). He doesn't seek what goes by the name of "immortality" (to be embalmed in Shakespeare Clubs and literary gazettes): "Let dignified oblivion, silence, and the vacant azure of Eternity swallow *me*; for any share of it, that, verily, is the handsomest, or one handsome way, of settling my poor account with the *canaille* of mankind, extant and to come." (Carlyle is always faithful to his moods and does not try to feign his feelings.)

## The Los Angeles Riots

*Aug. 14*: Three days of rioting in the Negro districts of Los Angeles. The National Guard called in. Negro comedian, Dick Gregory, shot in the thigh while trying to restrain the mob. Looting widespread, aimless, destructive. The young have learned enough to expect more from life than their quiet elders but aren't old enough to discipline their rebellion and to concentrate its power of opposition.

Chief of Police, William Henry Parker III, regarded as outstanding police administrator—an ultra-conservative. Attributes rioting to Supreme Court's civil rights decisions. He reports that riots began with somebody throwing rocks "and then, like monkeys in a zoo, others started throwing rocks." Negro leaders see riots as culmination of "years of economic frustration and police brutality." Parker blames them on gospel of civil disobedience preached by civil rights leaders. Most Negroes living in district are poorly paid blue-collar workers, an area of broken homes, debt, poverty, prostitution, drunkenness, narcotics.

See also a new book by a Negro who escaped from Harlem "stockade," Claude Brown,

*Manchild in the Promised Land* (Macmillan). This seems to be *Black Boy* brought up to date.

After a boyhood flecked with violence, thievery, jails, drugs (he's shot and sent to reform school), Brown ends up with a Howard University degree. He has studied law, learned to play the piano, but perhaps it was his courage and native intelligence that assured his survival.

## Sense and Disability

*John W. De Forest*: "Many a sensible man . . . has
saved up all his weakness for his choice of a wife."

"It is a matter of much satisfaction and gratitude
with me to observe how heroically most of us
endure the misfortunes of other people."

"It is not the great temptations that ruin us; it is
the little ones."

## A Sudden Blow

*Heraclitus*: "Every beast is driven to pasture by a blow."

## The Art of the One-Line Review

*Ambrose Bierce*: "The covers of this book are too far apart."

## Devaluing Everything

*Musil:* "[Arnheim] found in the soul a means of devaluing everything that his intellect could not master. For in this he is not different from his whole era, which had newly developed a strong religious tendency, not as the result of any religious destiny, but merely, as it seems, out of a feminine and irritable rebellion against money, knowledge, and calculation to all of which it passionately succumbed."

## On Death

I'm not one of those who, according to William
James, want to "cuddle up to death," but I should
like to survey Death respectfully, accustom
myself to his presence, stand within spying range,
live in peaceful coexistence with him during the
long truce. Then, when the time comes, I want
him to approach me not in the guise of an exe-
cutioner or a footpad but as a solicitous colleague
who will invite me to share his dark and revealing
knowledge.

## On Intelligence

*Paul Valéry*: Knowledge is really a potpourri of all the things we don't know, a stew of vague and crude scrutiny. "What was whole breaks down into parts; what was with us is against us. A slight turn of some mysterious screw shifts the microscope of consciousness, adds the element of time to increase the magnifying power of our attention, and finally brings our inner confusion into focus for us."

## Cavafy, "The City"

You said, "I will go to another land, I will go to
    another sea.
Another city will be found, a better one than this.
Every effort of mine is a condemnation of fate;
and my heart is—like a corpse—buried.
How long will my mind remain in this wasteland.
Wherever I turn my eyes, wherever I may look
I see black ruins of my life here,
where I spent so many years destroying and
    wasting."

You will find no new lands, you will find no other
    seas.
The city will follow you. You will roam the same
streets. And you will age in the same
    neighborhoods;
and you will grow gray in these same houses.
Always you will arrive in this city. Do not hope
    for any other—
There is no ship for you, there is no road.
As you have destroyed your life here
in this little corner, you have ruined it in the
    entire world.

## A Tale from Choate

This morning at coffee, Frank Ellis told me a true
story about a student at Choate.

The boy, 13 or 14 years old, an electronics bug,
very handy with the fascinating gadgetry of
batteries, two-way radios, microphones, etc.
For example, he had a tiny radio concealed in
an eyeglass frame and carried on conversations
*sotto voce* with a similarly equipped friend sitting
in another classroom. Even if experiments of this
kind were not permitted at Choate, he couldn't
resist the temptation to improvise *sub rosa*. He
constructed a TV set (strictly forbidden) and
placed it under his bed. Lying flat underneath
the bed, he would watch the screen fixed beneath
the springs.

For some reason (who knows what notion
prompted him—although I suspect it was a love
of mischief rather than viciousness), he decided
to bug the bedroom of one of his Masters in
the dormitory. The Master's wife—a pleasant
cookie-dispensing woman—was kind to him.
Apparently, he had no grudge against either.
What he didn't know, innocent though he was,
proved to be his spiritual undoing. The tapes
that he played back to himself recorded sounds,

conversations, etc. These revealed that the Master's wife was having an affair with another Master. Suddenly, the boy realized he was foundering in very deep water. How to get the equipment out of the bedroom? What to do about his disturbing knowledge? He had the luck or the good sense to call his father, who straightaway came to the school. Somehow the boy was able to extract the telltale and deadly paraphernalia. The story ends with father and son going out to the nearby woods arm-in-arm—a touching picture—and the father burning all the tapes in an expiating fire.

"Many men will recall how as boys they competed
to see who could create the highest urinary arc."

Sixty years ago, my back teeth
Floating in etherized beer,
I peed great arcs off train trestles,
Defeating peers in feats of urination.

Now a leaky hose reminds me of the jokes
We told when we were forceful spurters.

### A Visit to Edmund Wilson

*Jan. 3:* This morning, arose at seven, drank a cup
of coffee in the Wilson kitchen, and said good-
bye to Edmund and Elena. I had driven down on
a Saturday morning and spent the rest of the day
and Sunday in Wellfleet. Edmund looked feebler
than before and drank too much as usual, but
I found him gay and serene. He seems to enjoy
talking about literary matters and reminiscing
about his youth and his career in the '20s and '30s.
What started the conversation (which kept on
throughout my visit) was Sherman Paul's book.

He liked it in general (it's the first serious
full-length study of Wilson's career as writer,
critic, journalist, etc.), but he found it marred by
mistakes, omissions, false assumptions. Paul tried
to identify the characters in W's fiction and plays
and got them twisted. I told him that I thought
Paul's book was good, and he agreed, after telling
me he didn't think I'd like it.

We also discussed De Forest and some of the other
Civil War novelists. He didn't think Mark Twain
had much interest in the war but agreed that
my views might well be right. Mentioned two
words—"widdershins" and "deasil," discussed their
origin and meanings, the sinister implications of

"left" (*sinistra*) against "right," folk customs such as walking around church (*widdershins*). We got started on that subject after I told him about my word-collecting. He talked at some length about Compton Mackenzie, whose work he knows and admires. Advised me to read *Sinister Street*. Spoke of CM's remarkable vocabulary and read aloud from one of his novels in which unusual (not archaic) words were used with great appositeness and skill. One was "dwale"—"The sun's dwale." (*Dwale*: deadly nightshade (Scand.), so-called because it stupefies or dulls. In Danish means "trance," "torpor.")

Told me about Elaine Orr, first married to editor of *The Dial*, Scofield Thayer. Had child by E.E. Cummings while still married to Thayer. Divorced him (she was very rich) and married Cummings and more or less supported him. Classic beauty of the period. Came from Troy, N.Y. Her father owned a large shirt and collar factory. Many writers in love with her at the time. Dos Passos used her as model for the brittle "Elaine" in *Manhattan Transfer*. She divorced Cummings and married someone named McDermott. Wilson knew her well though never biblically. Cummings comments on Dos Passos when the two of them went to Spain after the war. Cummings always wanting to pick up girls, Dos Passos never; preferred to stay in best hotels. "Don't you ever dream of girls?" Cummings asks. "No," says DP. "What do you dream about then?" DP tells EEC that the previous night he dreamt that he had tried to get EEC to eat a bunch of asparagus.

Talk shifts to F. Crowninshield and Condé Nast. Former charming but unreliable, even unscrupulous. Ran *Vanity Fair* on short rung and underpaid staff. Wilson came to the magazine after Crowninshield fired Dorothy Parker. Robt. Benchley resigned in protest. The fired staff took no offense and kidded EW as a "scab." Condé Nast in 1920s: a Bennett Cerf type, smooth, well-dressed, a "plumber" (EW's term for a cocksman) and a "bounder." (EW still uses old-fashioned words occasionally. Told me that his father never swore but habitually expostulated with "Zounds!")

EW came to dislike Cummings excessively. Claimed that he never grew up and became more and more the narrow Bostonian, furious that his daughter had married a Roosevelt.

Wilson never worked for the Luce corporation and never wanted to. Refused a *Time* cover story.

Regards his Diary as the only valuable property
he can leave to his family. Only one volume ready.
Roger Straus has microfilmed whole Mss. Problem: much of it could embarrass the survivors and
their children and relations.

Takes pride in his professionalism. Likes what
Clifton Fadiman said of him, that he "worked
with his hands." His father didn't care what he
did. Simply asked him not to be a mediocrity.

## Bernard Malamud and the Hickses

*June 15*: Drive up to Hicks' for afternoon and evening. Granville pink and amiable but after closer look—drained of energy. Bernard Malamud & wife came to dinner. Looked less skull-like than he does in his pictures. Sprucely dressed; talkative wife. Very much according to a New York Jewish pattern. A bit self-important, even pompous in the way socially insecure people sometimes are. Without his pride as a writer and his fame, he would be undistinguished. Spoke about his new novel—"the most powerful thing I've ever written," a "wallop" in every chapter. Wondered how some young critic now writing a study of him could possibly do the job without reading this book. Thinks so much of it that he is currently doing a third draft. He is obviously a kind and generous man. Helps other writers. Probably moving to Cambridge for two years. Proud of his brainy son, a freshman at Yale. A good friend of Howard Nemerov, whom we both admire.

## Daniel's Dictionary

*Immane*: (Lat. *umanis*) very great, huge, vast.
Also monstrous in character, inhuman, atrocious.
[Archaic]: "so immane a man"—Chapman

*Nefandous*: (Lat. *nefandus*) not to be spoken,
unmentionable.

*Gallimatias*: mishmash, nonsense, farrago.
"Her talk is a gallimatias of several countries."
—Walpole

## Onward, Outward, Inward

*Erich Heller*: "He who is without a home in external reality will entrust himself to any wave of inwardness to take him anywhere—for anywhere may be the threshold of the mystery."

"Freedom is . . . impossible, for to be completely free would be to act without consequence. The child is 'free' in the sense that he is not conscious of consequence except in a very broad brute way: rewards and punishments, physical pain, etc.; but only heightened subjectivity complicates the number of possible consequences, makes them infinite, in fact, by adding the inner ones."

*DA's Reflections*: As we come to live inwardly rather than outwardly, the gulf widens between mind and matter. We hug our chimeras. More than that, we don't *see*. Children see. As we grow older, our vision blurs, or we gaze into ourselves rather than at the world.

What a tremendous pressure I feel to block out the daylight, and how easily one turns into one's self. We have reached the pitch of subjectivity today so that natural facts and artifacts are fantasy. What we seek in others is a reflection of our selves, our own need, our own hunger. We are mirror-people.

*Needed Today*: Artists who would restore the world to us once more and disappear by their own magic in the process. The greatest mystery is sunlight.

## The City in American Literature

A setting for Nightmare and Comedy, the approx-
imated Hell. In 1860s not much optimism. City
metaphor for disorder, violence. Later, writers
anatomize or fantasize. The city blurs into
suburbia. Stories in *New Yorker* by Peter De Vries,
Cheever, Updike. No more Albert Maltz, "Afternoon in the Jungle."

## The Vermillion Tips

*Charles White on Caucasians*: ". . . that nobly arched head, containing such a quantity of brain . . . ? Where that variety of features, and fullness of expression; those long, flowing graceful ringlets; that majestic beard, those rosy cheeks and coral lips? Where that . . . noble gait? In what other quarter of the globe shall we find that blush that overspreads the soft features of the beautiful women of Europe, that emblem of modesty, of delicate feelings . . . ? Where, except on the bosom of the European woman, two such plump and snowy white hemispheres, tipt with vermillion?"

## DA to DA

*Nov. 8*: Most books are gotten up, assembled, displayed. They have (the best ones) a glitter and form but no weight / diversity. A writer should feel "lightened" when he's done, as if his own substance has been incorporated into his brain-child. A good book impoverishes its author . . . You should write, as Wallace Stevens did, to cele-brate something—life, mystery, sensation. Today I drive V. S. Pritchett and Jonathan to New Haven.

## Daniel's Dictionary

*Slurry*: thin watery mud, or any substance resembling it. A cement or mortar used to repair furnace linings. The watery grindings from a grindstone.

(About the word "slurry," the *New Statesman* [1966] says, "[I]t is a horrible, powerful, Shakespearean word, almost too vivid and physical a folk creation, combining images of slime and hurry, slur and flurry, in one portmanteau concept.")

## Propaganda

*John Peale Bishop*: "Propaganda is aimed always at a group, actual or potential; it strives to affect men through what they have in common. Poetry answers a common purpose, appeals to man where he is most alone and most silent."

"Propaganda is a criticism of life by ideas; literature, a criticism of ideas by life."

*DA's Reflection*: And it might be added that the propagandist cannot waste his time by appealing to the private, the personal, the idiosyncratic, because time and economy require that he sweep the whole school into his sieve. Hence propaganda appeals to non-men or to the area beneath the neck—the gut, etc.

## On Dreiser's *An American Tragedy*

*Robert Penn Warren*: "[O]r it may be put that Clyde, having no sense of the reality of self, has no sense of the reality of others, and even his pity for others is always a covert self-pity."

**Gershom Scholem**

"But historical subjunctives are always illegitimate."

## On Criticism

*O. W. Firkins*: "Most judgments are not covered
by rules. The rules cover only the smallest part
of the ground. One-tenth of knowledge seems to
most men nine-tenths. Sensibility and common
sense are the properties on which criticism must
be based. When criticism is comprehensive and
verbose, it is a sign that criticism has ceased to be
authentic."

"A character is often better . . . for being normal
at the core and peculiar on the surface."

*On Hamlet*: "I am not sporting with paradox
when I say that the vice of insanity is that it
rationalizes everything at a stroke."

## On American Literature

*Tony Tanner*: To Hemingway, "life" or "existence"
means "now." He sees abstractions (life, death,
love, courage) as concretes—particular colors,
smells. Every one of his perceivers is over-
sensitized; they identify themselves with
material things. H's language is of necessity
the vernacular, the unliterary, for literary associations insulate the perceiving mind from reality.
His reality is plain—like rocks in clear water. He
removes the material that clutters. The anguish
of his tales and novels comes from the sense that
nothing exists beyond the senses. Better to live
a hundred years in ten seconds, to cram life, for
beyond is nothing. The moment of death for a
Hemingway hero "is the testing moment when
he is agonizingly poised between the wondrous
plenitude of the world and the oncoming smell
of bleak emptiness." H's goal: how to live in the
world, to relate in the environment. How to
see, to experience, to believe in the "essential
integrity of the senses." Only the concrete has
value. Ergo: the more one remembers clearly
and specifically, the more one has "lived." Most
people haven't because they've been distracted
by the irrelevant.

Tanner notes H's, and other American writers',

fondness for the paratactic, "the syntax which organizes and relates things by a variety of subordinate clauses." Also reveals the way a man "chooses to order his perceptions." Like Thoreau, H wants only the essential facts, not so much understatement but removal of the extraneous: the emotion itself, not what provoked it. Blurred writing is the cardinal sin, since it shows irreverence for the world and the "radical honesty of the eye." The "profundity of unseen detail." The writer who chooses the right detail will activate hundreds of unmentioned ones. H the conservationist of sensations too precious to hurry through.

## On Henry James

Do "words" for him derive from the "eye," or
from the reflecting mind behind it? James' writer
feels "the strain of observation and the assault of
experience," but the scrutiny of the eye continues throughout the process. The interfering
style is a direct aid to lucidity and provides the
author with an infinite number of ways to record
experience. In the Jamesian aesthetic, "rigidity,
inflexibility, intransigence" are bad characteris-
tics. Rigorous impositions are usually shown to
be ill-advised or cruel and always impoverishing.

*HJ and Hawthorne*: Apropos of "The Sacred
Fount," how HJ complicates the simpler para-
bles of Hawthorne and adds a social ambience.
Compare his narrator—observer, hoaxer, snooper—
with Henry Adams: Both are on the track of a
law that will reconcile disparate facts. Both guilty
of shaping these facts into a mystery. Both want
absolute certainty. For both (to quote Tanner out
of context), "only those things which cohere can
signify; the random, the contingent, the unre-
lated cannot yield up a meaning." Like Henry
Adams, the narrator not only sees horrors but also
likes them.

## History and Politics

*Paul Valéry*: Each of us is a cog in some larger entity or a series of entities, "surrendering to each of them a part of our self-ownership, and taking from each a part of our social definitions and our license to exist. We are all citizens, soldiers, taxpayers, men of a certain trade, supporters of a certain party, adherents of a certain religion, members of a certain organization, a certain club . . . we have become somehow quite well-defined entities. As such, we are now no more than objects of speculation, veritable *things*."

In sum, PV concludes, the Average Man may show any amount of reason and intelligence when he buys a car, even if swayed by symbolic status symbols. He wouldn't consult his priest. But when it comes to politics, foreign or domestic, the man falls back on the dank reservoir of old prejudiced opinions and slogans that require no thinking at all. Sellers of poisoned ideas don't list the ingredients.

"What is truly characteristic of history is that it plays a part in history itself." "The future, by definition, has no image. History provides us with the means to imagine it." History a kind of storehouse of situations, catastrophes, attitudes, decisions. Faced with crises, men don't consider crises something new: "rather they consult their imaginary memories." The search for precedent goes on. "History feeds on history."

**Daniel's Dictionary**

*Creodont*: any of the *creodonta*, a group of primitive carnivorous mammals characterized by small brains.

## An Item for a Mausoleum

*Pérez Galdós*: "[I]t was a weeping willow, one of those sentimental trees, which has had a more or less ceremonial part in every elegy committed since Rhetoric came into the world . . . and from its high spreading branches fell a rain of leaves, so delicate, faint, and suffering in appearance that they inspired a wish to give them smelling salts and bring them out of their poetic syncope . . . Such a willow was indispensable in an age in which the trees of romanticism had not yet turned into firewood."

*Alfred North Whitehead*: "Finally, there should
grow the most austere of all mental qualities;
I mean the sense for style. It is an aesthetic sense,
based on admiration for the direct attainment of
a foreseen end, simply and without waste. Style
in art, style in literature, style in science, style in
logic, style in practical execution have funda-
mentally the same aesthetic qualities, namely
attainment and restraint. The love of a subject
in itself and for itself, where it is not the sleepy
pleasure of pacing a mental quarter-deck, is the
love of style as manifested in that study."

"Here we are brought back to the position from
which we started, the utility of education. Style,
in its finest sense, is the last acquirement of the
educated mind; it is also the most useful. It per-
vades the whole being. The administrator with a
sense for style hates waste; the engineer with a
sense for style economises his material; the artisan with a sense for style prefers good work. Style
is the ultimate morality of the mind."

"But above style, and above knowledge, there is
a something, a vague shape like fate about the
Greek gods. That something is Power. Style is
the fashioning of power, the restraining of power.

But, after all, the power of attainment of the desired end is fundamental. The first thing is to get there. Do not bother about your style, but solve your problem, justify the ways of God to men, administer your province, or do whatever else is set before you."

"Where, then, does style help? In this, with style the end is attained without side issues, without raising undesirable inflammations. With style you attain your end and nothing but your end. With style the effect of your activity is calculable, and foresight is the last gift of gods to man. With style your power is increased, for your mind is not distracted by irrelevancies, and you are more likely to attain your object. Now style is the exclusive privilege of the expert. Who ever heard of the style of an amateur painter, of the style of an amateur poet? Style is always the product of specialist study, the peculiar contribution of specialism to culture."

## On Modern Drama

*O. W. Firkins*: "Apart from its primary demand for shudders, laughs, and kisses, the public requirements and exclusions are unfixed. With the reservation just made, there is hardly a virtue which the dramatist is forced to regard as indispensable; there is hardly an enormity which he is called upon to abjure as fatal. Art is the adjustment of conduct to conditions; it thrives on conditions. High conditions make high art; many conditions and sharp conditions make exact art. The reason why our commercial drama, having sacrificed everything to pleasure, succeeds so indifferently in the task of pleasing is that the demand which it has to meet is almost a demand for unconditional pleasure."

"Epigram shows us truth in the embrace of a lie."

## Never Blasé

*V.S. Pritchetts in Wellfleet, Jan. 28–30:* Drove
Victor and Dorothy Pritchett the 210 miles to
Wellfleet almost without stopping. Gray cold
day, flakes of snow. VSP in good form, chirruping
pleasantly throughout the trip and providing
the excellent company he invariably does. Both
Pritchetts enormously kind and tactful, born
travelers who notice keenly the oddities; never
blasé. We're welcomed by Elena and EW.

Wilson noticeably older—the dewlaps, the soften-
ing face, the profile less rocky. These last years of
hard work and drinking have weakened him (he's
about 72 now), and it's harder for him to pursue
a line of thought. He's just finished the first volume of his journals and has revised *I Thought of
Daisy*, which will be published along with a long
short story. Commented on the naiveté of Arthur
Schlesinger apropos of Arthur's recent article on
"Love in America." EW said that Arthur knows
nothing about artistic and Bohemian life in the
1920s and 1930s.

EW began to drink quite heavily about 5:30. By
dinnertime he'd become inarticulate, and after
dinner, unable to sustain any more talk, he went
to bed. We retired early.

Next morning I drove the VSPs around Wellfleet and down to our house and on to a roaring sea. Not yet high tide but the waves making great gouges in the collapsing dunes. Back to a good lunch and a little talk. Drove EW to Mary Meigs and the young French-Canadian girl's house. Barbara Deming away lecturing. The lesbian trio have been attacked and threatened by telephone and post after Barbara's return from Vietnam. EW invited "the girls" for drinks (against Elena's wishes). The pre-dinner drinks, the dinner, the after-dinner conversation all excellent. EW clear-headed and amusing. Ditto VSP. Topics discussed: Ed O'Connor's tax difficulties and income taxes in general; fiction of Walter Scott; Graham Greene, anecdotes about him; Cyril Connolly (VSP sees him as the incarnation of all the Seven Deadly Sins and specifies his differences with Stephen Spender); contemporary English playwrights; Spanish literature (EW refuses to read any of it; says it's too late and besides he doesn't think much of it). EW has decided not to undertake anything new. Will spend his last years reading the important writers he had had neither the time nor inclination to read (for example, Goethe, Scott, Balzac). VSP remarks as we drive home what a bookish man EW is. Discussion of Manchester's book on JFK. General agreement that it's a fascinating story told in a vulgar fashion. Manchester no writer. EW says that Mrs. Kennedy not very bright. Also says that he accepts the conspiracy theory of JFK's death.

Retire 11:00. Get up in snowstorm that, thank goodness, soon ends. Pleasant and fast return. Pritchetts pleased.

## DA's Obituary

D aniel Aaron
A rrived August 4, 1912
N amed after no one, in particular
I nvented nothing, except in words
E ven disposition
L oved a good deal and was loved

A nnounced early plans for old age
A ssisted various and sundry students
R etired at 65
O nce released
N ever heard of again

## Golden Presence

*DA*: Emerson's golden presence is everywhere,
and the poets who impatiently dash through
his golden mist—sometimes consciously, sometimes half aware—are flecked with his particles.
A hard man to dispose of—and easy to ridicule
and repudiate.

## 19th-Century American Hymn

I know that God is wroth with me,
  For I was born in sin;
My heart is so exceeding vile
  Damnation dwells therein.
Awake I sin, asleep I sin,

I sin with every breath;
When Adam fell he went to hell
  And damned us all to death.

## Young Folk

In 1967, it seems that all "activism"—Left, Right, and Center—is channeled into the mass media. Little is left to chance these days. No ideas are given time to incubate. How to avoid the TV channel, the magazine channel? Tom Hayden, one of the New Left participants, at YMHA. He's described in the *Hampshire Gazette* as a "resident activist" in Antioch. The Establishment is all-embracing so that protest music, drugs, etc. immediately become "subjects" to be "presented" and, in the process, "de-fanged."

Last night, the soothing voice of the announcer comments on the Young Folk who protest against life in America. This is good, he says: "We must learn what our young people are thinking about so that the differences between the generations will not widen excessively." There follows a young man's smooth rendition of a jumpy song of the wicked war & stupid old Johnson. What better way to funnel off the discontent. All over the U.S. young men and women are doing hard and often dangerous jobs and working, protesting, and going to jail.

## Daniel's Dictionary

*Appanage* (or *apanage*): (ML. *apanare*: to furnish with bread) land, or some other form of revenue, assigned for maintenance of a member of a family: whatever falls or belongs to one's rank or station in life. A natural or necessary accompaniment.

## Bridge over Troubled Waters

*Denis de Rougemont*: A sinvar bridge. "Of Manichean mythology, a bridge thrown across an infernal river, and one that only the elect are able to cross."

**Epitaph for an Advertising Man**
**(in the Dickinsonian Mode)**


I never excavated Why,
Explored the tomb of Whom,
But typed myself in triplicate—
A carbon-copied doom.

I read through libraries of woe
Researching They and We,
And now await inspection
From the Punctual Trustee.

## The New Left

*YMHA: Old Left vs. New Left. Former, Dick Rovere and Dwight Macdonald; latter, Ivanhoe Donaldson and Tom Hayden (March 6, 1967). Meeting Time 7:30. Chairman DA.*

I arrived on time, Donaldson and Hayden 20 minutes later. Brief discussion of subjects to be covered during evening panel.

Donaldson—smooth, cool, almost condescending. Struck me as a young man accustomed to the kindest solicitude and admiring attention. He was dressed in a very well-cut tweed jacket, black turtleneck sweater, slacks. He'd just flown in from California where he had addressed the students of San Jose. (He charged the same rate as V.P. Hubert Humphrey [$4000].) He languidly turned the pages of my questionnaire, suggested more questions, and then said that there was no such thing as a New Left, that the people who proposed this designation had no business doing so. Hayden now appeared—solemn, intense, melancholy. He hadn't looked at the list of questions either. Rovere and Dwight arrived 20 minutes before the panel began.

Some notes to remember if I ever write this up:

(1) Obviously, Hayden and Donaldson don't want to discuss the Old Left and had no intention of doing so.

(2) Their lack of interest could be attributed in part to their ignorance of it.

(3) For the benefit of the "Senior Citizens," they acknowledged that some men of the radical '30s had behaved well and were part of the American radical heritage, but these "heroes" were unknown and unsung.

(4) No indication that Hayden or Donaldson were curious about the fate of their predecessors. The important point to consider was why radical movements had failed, but Hayden saw no discrepancy between the burden of this question and his own ahistorical attitude.

(5) The "young radicals," in short, used the occasion to sermonize on American Evil and to express their anger and contempt for their critics. Dwight's sometimes flippant but not ill-natured animadversion infuriated them. They twice described when he accused them of not reading and of speaking foolishly on occasion, although

he did commend their idealism and say that he shared their disgust for much going on in and outside of America. Still he described their activities as a "Children's Crusade."

(6) Donaldson & Hayden allergic to criticism and can tolerate only those who cheer them on. Not concerned with persuading others to accept their views. They preach. They announce. If you "dig," all right; if you don't, you're not salvageable anyway. Kicked off the Reservation, you become They, not the Enemy.

(7) My first hard unvarnished look at the New Intransigence, the mystical Narodniki and their Youth Claque—proud, priestly, humorless, melancholy—committed to doom and failure—and relishing their role.

## Mrs. Chesnut's Diary

David Donald suggests that I read Mrs. Chesnut's
chronicle of Civil War years, which he sees as a
novel. No ms. extant. One suspects retrospective
interpolations in many passages. (I may sometime do the same thing in my journals, using
the journalistic outline to provide the structure
for subsequent reconsiderations.) Her facts may
be softened or transmogrified by distance. All
the same, Mrs. C. an instinctive novelist. Her
position in the Confederate elite, and her duties,
may have prevented her from undertaking
anything more literary than her diary, but she
was obviously an intellectual, a kind of Southern
Jane Austen: no sentimentality, cant—a sharp and
witty perceiver, enjoyer of gossip, even, possibly,
of the broad jokes she deprecates in her diary.
Her diary not kept in secret. She knows that it
will be read (as it was by her friends).

### Daniel's Dictionary

*Tansy*: a coarse strong-scented herb with toothed plumate leaves and corymbs of yellow flowers—native to Old World & common weed in N. America.

*Funambulist*: tightrope walker.

## The Fifth Dilution

*Santayana*, Letters: "May not the remarkable sloppiness and feebleness of the cultivated American mind be due to this habit of drinking life in its fifth dilution only? What you need is not more criticism of current authors, but more *philosophy*: more courage and sincerity in facing nature directly, and in criticizing books or institutions only with a view to choosing among them whatever is most harmonious with the life you want to lead."

*Santayana*, The Last Puritan: "Not only was America the biggest thing on earth, but it was soon going to wipe out everything else; and in the delirious dazzling joy of that consummation, he forgot to ask what would happen afterwards."

*Santayana*, The Last Puritan: "Besides, black in itself has a function and beauty more recondite than white has, and deeper. It is the ultimate background of space and of consciousness, satisfying intrinsically, and by contrast a source of precision and loveliness in other colors. It tires less, it protects more . . ."

### Daniel's Dictionary

*Calefactory*: a vessel for warming hands, before administering the Eucharist. A warm room in a monastery.

*Buckeen*: (Irish) a young man of the middle class or lower aristocracy who copies the practices of wealthier people.

*Dulse*: coarse, edible, red seaweed. "The middle sea contains no crimson dulse."—Thoreau

*Preconize*: (Lat. *praecox*: crier, herald) (1) to proclaim, command publicly. (2) To summon publicly. (3) To declare solemnly.

*Gnarly*: like a gnarled limb on the chopping block, complicated and knotted, hard to understand—not gratuitously mean like an "ornery" man—but difficult.

## With the Right Crowds

"Flock" of sheep, "herd" of cattle, "bevy" of
quail and larks, "covey" of partridges, "drove"
of hogs, "school" of fish, "swarms" of robbers,
"shoal" of porpoises, "gang" of ruffians, "mob"
of bargain-hunters, "bunch" of flowers, carrots,
and crooks.

*Suggested alternatives*: a "bunch" of bottles,
a "drove" of politicians, a "school" of ruffians,
a "shoal" of children, "gang" of teachers or rabbits,
"herd" of pilgrims, "swarm" of priests, "troop" of
dolphins.

*April 8*: A week ago, Sunday, President Johnson declared that he would not be a candidate for re-election. This came after an unctuous and irritating apologia about his intentions and accomplishments followed by his decision to halt bombing of North Vietnam (cities, unfortified areas) and to keep U.S. planes below the demilitarized zone or only to bomb military concentrations. The part about his political withdrawal came almost as an afterthought. Many listeners, bored or disgusted with White House drivel, had already turned off their sets.

The next day, LBJ took it from both sides—especially from Fulbright, who felt LBJ hadn't gone far enough and that his gesture would provoke no response except angry and contemptuous comment. But Fulbright had to eat his words. Hanoi did reply. The Stock Market zoomed. Most people see Robert Kennedy as the chief beneficiary. On Thursday, Martin Luther King assassinated. The response to his death has been as earth-shaking as—perhaps more so than—JFK's. Prompted by what? Guilt, fear, compassion? A belated recognition that a saint has been living among us unsuspected. At this very moment, a funeral is being conducted in Atlanta attended by thousands—diplomats & sundry of the eminent and extraordinary, as if this man's death has shifted a huge weight and cleansed the offal of a nation. One sees that something has happened, that the country is now on a different tack. These assassinations are interpreted in Europe and elsewhere as the acts of a deranged and vicious people. We treat them as inadvertent prods to virtue.

## Robert Kennedy Assassination

Arrived in L.A. evening of the assassination and
in the Ambassador Hotel when the shooting
occurred. How many years have passed since
I was in that now beat-up and tawdry hotel?
I grew up only a few blocks from Wilshire Blvd
and Fifth and played in the excavations when
the hotel was being built. Now I was back to be
present at a murder.

Eleanor [DA's sister-in-law] and I didn't hear
the shots. We'd left the ballroom only minutes
before to see what the Birchites and other kooks
were doing at the Rafferty headquarters, and it
was only after leaving the hard-faced grimacing
celebrators that we learned that some horror
had happened elsewhere in the hotel. Hysterical
moaning young girls, cries of "He's dead! He's
dead!" And then mobs of people, many completely out of control, weeping or crying, some in
a trance. Unable to leave because of a police edict,
we stayed for a few more hours and gradually
patched out the facts.

Some dream lines composed last night:

> Come dance with me,
> Come dance upon the snow.
> I'll feed you fireflies
> To set you all aglow.

*Anlage*: an inherited predisposition to certain traits or particular character development.

*Anamnesis*: sudden consciousness of innate knowledge one didn't know one possessed.

*Culch*: stones, old shells, etc., furnishing points of attachment for the spawn of oysters. Also rubbish or refuse.

*Shroff*: in India a banker or money-changer; expert to detect counterfeits.

## Gratification

Asked if he weren't gratified by the attention he'd received at an evening gathering of celebrated literary people, Dr. Johnson replied: "No, sir, not highly gratified; yet I do not recollect to have passed many evenings with fewer objections."

## Awful Divinity

*Thackeray to His Mother:* "So with our diseases—
we die because we are born; we decay because
we grow. I have a right to say, 'O, Father, give me
submission to bear cheerfully (if possible) and
patiently my sufferings': but I can't request any
special change in my behalf from the ordinary
processes, or see any special Divine *animus* super-
intending my illnesses or wellnesses. Those people seem to me presumptuous who are for ever
dragging the Awful Divinity into a participation
with their private concerns . . . Brother Jones
writes of Brother Brown how preciously he has
been dealt with: Brown has been blessed by an illness; he has had the blessing of getting better; he
has relapsed, and finally has the blessing of being
called out of the world altogether. I don't differ
with Brown essentially—only in the compliments,
as it were, which he thinks it is proper to be for
ever paying. I am well: Amen. I am ill: Amen.
I die: Amen always. I can't say that having a tooth
out is a blessing—is a punishment for my sins.
I say it's having a tooth out."

"Old Age"

When skin
Gets paper thin,
Scratches bleed.

I heed
These hints—
And wince.

## Hugo von Hofmannsthal

"Children are entertaining because they are easily entertained."

"Self-love and self-hate are the deepest of all earthly creative powers."

"Powerful imaginations are conservative."

"The nearer the scholar or thinker approaches (without becoming) the artist, the more dubious a phenomenon he becomes."

"Spirit is transcended reality. What absents itself from reality is not spirit."

"Not to know many things but to bring many things into contact with one another is a first step toward the creative."

"Forms animate and kill."

"To approve is more difficult than to admire."

"It's an unpleasant but necessary art to keep the vulgar at bay by coldness. 'Only the cold,' runs an Arabian proverb, 'prevents dung from soiling your feet.'"

"At the beginning of life we are most subjective and least understand subjectivity in others."

"The hesitation to speak to another of one's own personal concerns is a self-warning of the soul; into each confession, each account, distortion easily enters, turning in a trice the most delicate, most sacred, into something vulgar."

"In the more refined forms of human relations, even in marriage, nothing should be taken for granted, nothing considered permanent, but everything considered a gift of each single world-encircling moment."

"The blending of the descriptive with the enthusiastic produces an intolerable style."

"Naturalism distorts Nature because by copying the surface it has to neglect the wealth of inner relatedness—Nature's real mysterium."

## Omens

*Allen Tate*: "Omens are those signals of futurity that we recognize when the future has already slid into the past."

## Daniel's Dictionary

*Fizgig*: a frivolous giddy woman. A firework that produces a sputter sound. (Related to obsolete *fise*: to break wind, to fart.)

## Matherisms

Cotton Mather describes the "witch"—Goodwife Glover—as "crazed in her intellectuals."

## Overestimations

*Oscar Wilde*: "No one survives being over-estimated, nor is there any surer way of destroying an author's reputation than to glorify him without judgment and to praise him without tact."

## Underestimations

*Oscar Wilde*: "He is a trifle cynical, this friend, and decidedly pessimistic. Of him it was reported that he never believed in anything until he saw it, and then he was convinced it was an optical illusion."

## Daniel's *Pomes*

Haiku ("Self-Abjuration")

Don't let go, old leaf.
Hang on to the withered branch
Till spring: then float down.

*June 11*: Edmund Wilson died today. Call from Helen Muchnic. He was in Talcottville and planning to drive down to Cummington. Burial service at Wellfleet. EW had ordered the text (third book of Ecclesiastes) in John Knox's bony and harsh translation. Also the 90th Psalm turned out to be EW's last lecture to his contemporaries— this one from the other side. A bleak hedonistic assertion: What do we know of the afterlife? Or of this life, where the wicked prosper? Best cling to what you know, do your work, aim for commendations and rewards now.

**Daniel's Dictionary**

*Hermeneutics*: science and methodology of interpretation, esp. of scriptural texts. (So one could rightly speak of Marxist hermeneutics.)

*Soteriology*: (Gk. *sotirion*: deliverance) theoretical doctrine of salvation.

*Haetal*: in India a halting of work or business; a strike or boycott.

# The Canon

*Richard Porson on Southey's* Thalaba: One of those poems "which will be read when Homer and Virgil are forgotten, but not till then."

## Poetasters

Stott, early 19th-c. poetaster satirized by Byron in "English Bards and Scotch Reviewers." When the reigning family left Portugal, he composed an ode beginning with the lines:

"Princely offspring of Braganza,
Erin greets thee with a stanza."

He also wrote a sonnet on rats and "a most thundering ode" including these lines:

"Oh! For a lay! Loud as the surge
That lashes Lapland's sounding shore."

## Troubles

*Julian Hawthorne, Quoting His Father*: "Troubles . . .
are a sociable sisterhood; they love to come
hand-in-hand or sometimes, even, to come side
by side, with long-looked-for and hoped-for
good-fortune."

Ralph Ellison sees my book *The Unwritten War*
as proof positive that American writers were
afflicted by a collective racial myopia.

## Nixon Speaks on Watergate

*April* 30: Blames the Democratic Party for pro-
voking a few of his over-zealous henchmen. No
White House officials involved. "I love America.
God bless each and every one of you." The President stumbled over the word "integrity."

## Daniel's Dictionary

*Smorzando* [lovely word]: a fading away.

*Morendo*: gradual diminuendo at the end of a
movement.

*DA's Reflection*: So I should use "smorzando" as a
temporary fading with the likelihood of renewal
and "morendo" as final death. We have many
*smorzandos* but only one *morendo*.

## On Miracles

Jere Whiting quotes the words of a Maine fisherman to a boaster: "You can do wonders and shit 'Miracles.'"

## Four Lines from the Fiction of Sax Rohmer

"My man, reclothe your indecently nude person."
"Are you admiring my justly celebrated legs?"
"I speak all kinds of English. Tell me which kind
      you prefer."
"Zoe Oppner entered the room, regally carrying
      her small head."

## Edgar Wind on Madness and Splendor

". . . by moving into the margin art does not lose
its quality as art; it only loses its direct relevance
to our existence: it becomes a splendid super-
fluity." (Applies to religious literature as well.)

". . . for it is essential to the well-being of society
that the whole should be less mad than the parts."

Plato "thought a man could be transformed by
the things he imagined."

Jacob Burckhardt defined mediocrity "as the truly
diabolical force in the world."

"If the Greeks had not been so responsive to
an exquisite phrase or a beautiful gesture, they
might have judged a political oration by its truth
and not by the splendour with which it was deliv-
ered: but their sobriety was undermined by their
imagination."

"Great ideas have a way of either quickening or
clogging the spirit of a painter."

"Is it really true that there are more bad didactic
poems than, say, bad poems on love, or bad patri-
otic or religious hymns?"

"The isolation, which we think of as essential to artistic creation, has been pushed to the point where artists cerebrate far too much because they are in need of thoughts and those for whom thinking is primary business do not supply them."

"Great works of art . . . are as tough as they are fragile."

"The antithesis between modern engineering and medieval spirituality is one of those facile and fallacious disjunctions by which we get trapped when we regard art as naturally opposed to mechanization."

"The complaint against mass distribution of art is not that it serves too many people, but that it serves them badly . . . It is not the number of persons who look at art that is alarming, it is the number of works of art they look at, and the reduction of art to a passing show."

"Picasso's method of breaking up natural forms becomes literal-minded when he applies it to forms that are actually broken."

## Black Wedding

*Sept. 7*: I met the mother of my student Robert, as well as his imminent father- and mother-in-law. Also a friend who's getting a degree in psychology at the University of Minnesota.

Wedding opens with an "African dance"—a half-dozen girls, 12–14, dressed in long skirts, their hair coiled in braids. Drums beat as the procession of main participants moved in time toward the pulpit. In his address, the minister committed the pair to God and Africa and enjoined them to be strong & beautiful & Black. Christ and God not ignored but play a minor role. A small chorus of children sing, naturally and engagingly, a song (Swahili?) & they are followed by an adult chorus after the Benediction. They sing, "You are my sunshine." Finally, a prayer and a jumping hymn. Exit the principals accompanied by clapping hands.

N.B. Event took place in the Afro-American Methodist Episcopal Church, Austin St. Central Square, Cambridge (the first Black wedding that I've attended). Time, Sept. 7, 1973. Saturday, 3 o'clock p.m. About 150 of the guests dressed in African garb. Robert himself wore an elegant caftan and circular headpiece.

## On Aging

*Sir Peter Medawar:* "It is very doubtful . . . if a true distinction of principle can be drawn between the process of aging and these to her more obviously adventitious misfortunes, for aging itself is the outcome of a long series of covert mishaps and physiological misadventures: no one of them singly fatal but sufficient in their sum to produce that slow deterioration of the faculties which we recognize as aging. Thus there is no rational case for discouraging or prohibiting research on aging."

## Daniel's Dictionary

*Multinefarious*: my word for Pres. Nixon's activities, or perhaps that's a little unfair.

## Apply Now to Money-Bags

*Nov.* 30: Now that my book is out (*The Unwritten War*)—the reviews not bad, not ecstatic—the time has come to look ahead and face up to the old obstacles, personal and professional. Harvard not deadening (I glimmer more brightly, perhaps, in its coruscations), but duties become excessive as the grid of responsibility thickens and widens. I still move with ease through the warp and woof, but every day more filaments are cast out to ensnare me. So the need for a break, a new plan, a new book, research—and a grant. Apply now to the Money-bags.

But for what? My idea for the Chardon Street meetings is still uppermost, but I see the neces-sity of doing a certain amount of digging even to make the project clear to me &, much more, to those who will judge my applications. Probably the safest way would be to present a project more general in scope than the Boston occasion of 1840–41, and to look at the entire reform move-ment in antebellum America. I have in mind something like *Enthusiastic Temperaments* or *The Temperament of Enthusiasm: A Study of the Reform-ist Personality*. That has a nice ring to it. I should concentrate on personalities and events, probe the journals and letters that might cast new light

on both. The Civil War doesn't asphyxiate the
Enthusiasts but creates a climate less receptive to
transcendental aims. The Chardon Street people
were confident or, more to the point, un-uniformed
and unharnessed. I really know little about them,
how they wrote and thought. Did they have precious parts that went unnoticed? Emerson a key
figure. He had the wit and wisdom to savor them,
and his benevolent response to the crowds of
radicals and cranks (he recognized a part of himself in every type and cause) is instructive. The
Establishment writers and intellectuals judged
them externally—and more superficially too.

## Half-Dream Verse

*Dec. 3*: "When Adolf Hitler listened to / *Ein Heldenleben* by Richard Strauss / He was as quiet as a mouse."

## My Astrological Chart

*LEO.* "Leos are charming, entertaining, genuinely appealing, with a show-biz streak that could zoom to the top this January. Some people will find you a show-off . . . others will think you delightful."

## Anniversary of M. L. King's Death

I note from the excerpts of essays of black students in NYC that King is already passing into myth. The gist of the responses: if King were alive, people of all races would love one another, crime and violence of all sorts would disappear from the streets. Corruption in government, oil shortages—all the present evils—would no longer afflict us.

One word describes it: "Splendid."

### "Liberal"

Current associations: smooth, accommodat-
ing, unctuous, undaring, sitting-on-both-sides.
"Liberalism" a disguise for a malign faith, whereas
"Libertarian" has strong, bold, downright old-
fashioned ring.

## Zealots

*Rebecca Harding Davis*: "The man who rebels against an established rule, from Absalom to Paderewski, feels that he must wear his hair down his back. The man who makes war upon the world's great ordinances always picks a quarrel with its harmless little habits, even decencies."

## Qualifications

*Hazlitt on Critic William Gifford*: "He is admirably qualified for this situation, by a happy combination of defects, natural and acquired."

## The Young

*John Peale Bishop*: "A romantic immorality must
return whenever civilization is found no longer
an aid but a hindrance to the accomplishment
of desires. The alternative is asceticism. A protest
was bound to be made by a generation in which
the individual had suffered so much from society
and suffered, as he felt, under the most false pretenses . . . Romantic emotions reappear in every
generation and always at that moment when the
young first conceive their own annihilation.
At that moment, regardless of the state of society
in which they find themselves, there follows an
assertion of whatever they conceive to be in their
own right. This consciousness is enhanced for the
young to whom death is continuously present,
as in war."

## Your Great Friendly Computer

*A Phrase from an Avis Advert:* How cozy and comfortable to know that your GFC (like the Wise Old Doctor and the Old Family Lawyer) has you in its mind come hell or high water; that it can never grow senile; that you are banked in its capacious elastic brain. Your GFC is a friend to all—to bureaucrats, the police, and credit companies. You will never be alone or forgotten. And you must be open and candid with the GFC, ready to confess all, to hide nothing. It will make life easier for you.

## Exercise in the Sounds "st" and "sts"

Amidst the mists,
   With stoutest boasts,
He thrusts his fists

   Against the posts
And still insists
   He sees the ghosts.

## Speken Propurly

"Of Paradys ne can Not I speken propurly: for I was not there." —*The Travels of Sir John Mandeville*

## Curative Décor

*Edith Wharton to Mary Berenson:* "I believe I know the only cure [for despair], which is to make one's centre of life inside of one's self, not selfishly or calculatingly, but with a kind of unassailable serenity—to decorate one's inner house so richly that one is content there, glad to welcome any one who wants to come and stay, but happy all the same in the hours when one is inevitably alone."

## Edith Wharton Once Referred to German Tourists

as "Ja-Hoos."

## Daniel's Dictionary

*Hypnopompic*: "of or pertaining to the partially conscious state preceding complete awakening." The unsealed consciousness between sleep and awakening that Keats refers to—source of pictures, ideas, fancies dredged up from the unconscious and not yet obliterated by the light of awakening or spoiled by exposure to sunlight.

*Briggady*: feisty, uppity.

*Rebarbative*: repellant, irritable, unattractive, literally "to face beard to beard."

*Ostrakon*: shell-hard; from which "ostracized" derives. Greeks voted for ostracism by casting shells.

*Inquiline*: dweller living in another's burrow.

## Current Expressions

"You can say that again!" and "You'd better believe it."

## Puritan Prayer

"Lord, cast me down I pray thee to the ground in my received self (I, that which is called I, or myself), and kill this self of mine through thy death; do thou overcome in me self (or I, or I hood, or I ness, that which we mean when we say 'it's I'); cast my whole self down to the ground in thy death."

## Natural Bourne Sympathies

*Randolph Bourne*: "I love people of quick, roving intelligence, who carry their learning lightly, and use it as a weapon to fight with, as handles to grasp new ideas with, and as fuel to warm them into a sympathy with all sorts and conditions of men."

The critic Bourne called for would rectify "the uncritical hospitality of current taste" and provide "an intelligent, pertinent, absolutely contemporaneous criticism, which shall be both precise and severe and encouraging . . ." and set to work to discover and interpret in others the motives and values and efforts he feels in himself. Such criticism was not "merely appreciative" but took into account "ideas and social movements and the intellectual and spiritual colors of the time." Bourne demanded a "new classicism" requiring "power with restraint, vitality with harmony, a fusion of intellect and feeling, and a keen sense of artistic conscience." (RB's ideal critic an amalgam of Pound, Eliot, and Edmund Wilson.)

## In Aboriginal Australia

*From Newspaper Clipping*: "The sacred green ant, revered by the aborigines of Australia's remote north, is holding up plans to mine the world's richest uranium deposit."

"The ore, buried just beneath the scorched landscape, is less than 200 yards from an area known in aboriginal legend as Gabo-Diang (the dreaming place of the green ants). The aborigines believe the half-inch-long ants at Gabo-Diang are descendants of the godlike great green ant, one of the spiritual beings who established all the patterns of human life and can still influence them for good or ill."

## Biographical Violations

A man writes what he calls a "Current Autobiography." An account of his life, personality,
thoughts all emerge inadvertently as he reflects
on the well-known people of his times—artists,
teachers, professional men—the "celebrities" he
knew or was introduced to or "almost met" or
who knew friends who knew friends, etc.

At first the "I" is a pale reflection known only for
his tenuous connection with the "known," but
gradually & cumulatively his mind and character
begin to take shape and deepen. He studies the
"known" more searchingly and reveals himself as
he reveals others. In the process his own life is
disclosed in patches, chronology violated. The
autobiography turns out to be accounts of people
(alphabetically presented) who directly or indi-
rectly figured in his "history"—people in the news.
The autobiographer-cum-biographer becomes
the historian/novelist whose subject is his own
work and his times.

## "Easy Aces": Jane and Goodman Ace

New York Times, *Nov. 13*: "The couple received network status on CBS in 1931 and moved to NBC in the next year. Their show was built on what Mr. Ace maintained was his wife's natural aptitude for malapropisms. Such expressions as 'a ragged individualist,' 'words of one cylinder,' 'we're insufferable friends.' 'Congress is still in season' delighted listeners. Other 'Jane-isms' were 'You could have knocked me down with a feather,' 'Home wasn't built in a day,' 'The Ten Amendments,' 'Up at the crank of dawn,' and 'The fly in the oatmeal.'"

### Killing Rats

"Zinc phosphide . . . induces vomiting, and since the rat has no throat mechanism that allows it to vomit, the strain of trying causes a heart attack or kidney failure," according to Solomon Peoples, the deputy director of the Department of Pest Control Bureau, who is responsible for the super-rat blitz.

## Stylistic Fatigue

*John Sterling to Thomas Carlyle*: "But a style may be fatiguing and faulty precisely by being too emphatic, forcible and pointed; and so straining the attention to find its meaning, or the admiration to appreciate its beauty."

## Our British Ladies

Dugald Stewart quotes a sentence from
Addison to illustrate the danger of using
figurative language. "This much I thought
fit to premise before I resumed the subject
I have already handled. I mean the naked
bosoms of our British ladies."

## On Carlyle's Achievement

*G.K. Chesterton:* "His supreme contribution, both to philosophy and literature, was his sense of the sarcasm of eternity. Other writers had seen the hope or the terror of the heavens; he alone saw the humor of them. Other writers had seen that there could be something elemental and eternal in a song or statue; he alone saw that there could be something elemental and eternal in a joke."

## Emily Dickinson & the Chickens of Death

Commentators harp on her obsession with Death, but a look at any family correspondence anywhere in the U.S. at her time would show the same preoccupation with health, sickness, and death. What's important is what she made of it.

One of her many phrases for the grave: "This slim palace in the dust." During a funeral service she attended, chickens fluttered from their coop into the church: "I suppose the dead lady used to feed them, and they wanted to bid her good-by."

## Seasonal Dickinson

"The summer has been wide and deep, and a deeper autumn is but the Gleam concomitant of that waylaying light."

"The noons are more laconic and the sundowns sterner, and Gibraltar lights make the village foreign. November always seemed to me the Norway of the year."

"Who could be ill in March, that month of Proclamation? Sleigh bells and Jays contend in my Matinee, and the North surrenders, instead of the South, a reverse of Bugles."

## Politics According to Dickinson

Why does ED call herself "Queen"? Why the
royal "we" in her poems and letters? Because she
is the bride of Christ ennobled by her suffering?
(To follow Christ is to take the "royal way." The
words of the Bible "are great bars of sunlight in
many a shady heart.")

"George Washington was the father of his country—
George Who?"

*In Sum*: Truth must be told slant and "dazzle
gradually" else "every man be blind." ED can
be likened to a kite attached to a copper wire.
She sails up into the electrical immensity, and
through her the gods discharge their coded
messages. She bounces against the boundaries
of Circumference, receives heavenly bulle-
tins and records divine/malign/benign. ED as
Register of Bolts. A coy impresario of Electrical
Displays: ED as "world," Nature the transmission
belt.

## DA Reflects on ED

From out her windowed citadel
She looked at life askant—
Decoding Messages from Up—
Recording them in slant—

To couch a cryptic Bulletin
In hard prismatic verse—
Refracts the Glare of Majesty—
Invalidates Remorse.

## Uncertainty

*Emily Dickinson*: "Hamlet wavered for all of us."

## The Inestimable Alice James

*On Colossal Vanity*: Alice James notes that it is from Colossal Vanity that "springs all the grotesque in life." She refers to herself as an "unsentimental spinster" and jeers at death—which of course reveals her covert respect for the Great Prince.

*On Spiritualists*: "I suppose the thing 'medium' has done more to degrade spiritual conception than the grossest forms of materialism or idolatry: was there ever anything transmitted but the pettiest, meanest, coarsest facts and details: anything rising above the squalid intestines of human affairs? And oh, the curious spongy minds that sop it all up and lose all sense of taste and humour!"

*On the Church*: But Alice James sings her mortuary airs *con brio*. Two English ladies told her that they regretted that HJ Senior did not know "the Broad Catholic Church" (described by AJ as "the centimetre of washed-out Anglican Evasions").

*On Superstition*: AJ blesses HJ Sr. (the "delicious infant, who couldn't submit even to the thralldom of his own whim") for threshing "out all the ignoble superstitions," the dry husks, "so that we had not the bore of wasting our energy in raking over and sweeping out the rubbish."

*On God & Eternity*: "One cries out, bowed down in supplication, for strength, but how can any creature measure her judgment with that of the Doer of Good, how can she propose to make her paltry necessities an element for modification of another's destiny, how can she thrust her miserable plaints in the presence of Majestic Death?"

*On a Genteel Impoverished Lady*: "On this little heap of social ruin, however, the gentlewoman was impregnably entrenched, and how often have I gazed sadly through her atmosphere of inherited good breeding, and seen unfold itself the endless row of desperate ciphers, by which she is multiplied on this teeming island."

*AJ Invalided in England & Yearns for America*: "What a tide of homesickness swept me under for a moment! What a longing to see a shaft of sunshine shimmering thro' the pines, breathe in the resinous air and throw my withered body down upon my mother earth, bury my face in the coarse grass, worshipping all that the ugly, raw emptiness of the blessed land stands for— the embodiment of a Huge Chance for hemmed in Humanity! Its flexible conditions stretching and lending themselves to all sizes of man; pallid

and naked of necessity; undraped by the illusions
and mystery of a moss-grown, cobwebby past,
but overflowing with a divine good-humour and
benignancy—a helping hand for the faltering, an
indulgent thought for the discredited, a heart of
hope for every outcast of tradition."

*On Episcopalianism*: It has neither the "historical splendour of the Catholic Church to lend
it romance and authority nor the grim heroic
nudity of austere and masculine Calvinism to
brace the mental and moral sinews."

## Richard Hofstadter's Last Days

My sense of his resentment and panic, his look of a man deserted and betrayed, of one who had already crossed over and was looking at the stupidly alive from the other side of the Styx.

Such men (I quote Avery Weisman) "are dependent, without trusting in their right to be cared for; they are without confidence in their reality testing because, in some inscrutable sense, they are already gone . . . Even experienced professionals find themselves withdrawing in the presence of death, and many well-meaning people feel a natural revulsion. The sights and smells of terminal disease are just as disgusting as the thought of death is horrendous. There is often an infectiousness about the deadly atmosphere that cannot help but arouse antipathy and aversion. There are no effective sprays and deodorants for the stench of despair."

*DA's Reflection*: In making your final exit, don't dash awkwardly off the stage in a panic. Walk. Don't run.

**Nicholas von Hoffman**

*On Aristotle Onassis*: "For him, the world was to loot. He said, 'My favorite country is the one that grants maximum immunity from taxes, trade restrictions and unreasonable regulations,' which is no country at all. It follows that this patriot fathered the supertanker, that dreadful ship with the capacity to pollute seas and oceans, our common international inheritance. Had they scattered his ashes on the waters, it would have created a 10,000-square-mile oil slick."

*On the Late Chief Justice Warren*: "The late Chief Justice Earl Warren is quoted as calling former President Nixon 'a cheat, a liar and a crook,' in an article by Alden Whitman of the *New York Times* . . . Whitman says that Warren often referred to his successor, Chief Justice Warren E. Burger, as 'a horse's ass.'"

Whitman reports that "Warren detested Nixon with 'unjudicious choler.'" According to Whitman, "Warren told him that 'Tricky is perhaps the most despicable President this nation has ever had . . . and he brought my country which I love into disrepute. Even worse than abusing his office, he abused the American people.'"

## Souring of S. J. Perelman

*DA*: The wild elation of *Vinegar Puss* now gone, and the pessimism and venom suppressed in his first pieces are coming out openly—the old embittered man, full of hate for the country which once struck him (as it had Mark Twain and Mencken) as an endlessly entertaining circus and zoo.

## Vegetarians

*Judy Klemesrud*: "Not long ago, vegetarians were viewed by many people as weird, wiry crusaders for carrot juice who ran around in tennis shoes rather than wear the leather of some animal's back." Once they kept their eating habits to themselves. Nowadays they're much more vocal.

## Morbidity

*J. G. Huneker*: "But the suggestion of morbidity may be found in the writings of every great writer from Plato to Dante, from Shakespeare to Goethe: it is the faint spice of morbidity that lends a stimulating if sharp perfume to all literature."

## Noon

The hungry clock clasped its hands. It was time to eat.

## Badinage

Eternal Revenue Bureau (Heaven)

Mozeltov Cocktail (birthday drink)

Warping and woofing, the dogs tapestried the air
with balls of howls.

Groves of whispering women

Shakespeare blew himself up and became his
own characters.

Now I know why I was born: to be beguiled by
Handel's horn.

## Proverbs

*(Spanish) Santayana*: "Man has two childhoods, one means life and the other death, but in both he has a jolly time."

*(Russian), Quoted by Randall Jarrell*: "Heaven gives us habits to take the place of happiness."

*Lucretius*: "You may live to complete as many generations as you will; nevertheless, that everlasting death will still be waiting."

*Livy*: "We can endure neither our vices nor the remedies for them."

Herald-Tribune, *Jan. 6*: "With older institutions falling into contempt, and the new men—always better organized than informed—pressing for instant cornucopias, liberal and conservative politicians composed their differences. To hold off the conflicting demands of their petulant constituencies, they tried to save themselves in the debt, central control and adventurism that we today have no difficulty recognizing."

## Don King's Guardian Angels

The Miami News, *March 28*: "With his inim-
itable vocabulary, Don King once publicly thanked
Lombardo for helping in the Ali-Wepner match."

"'When I was running the foot race of time,'
King said of his angel, 'he stopped the bell from
tolling. He came with his checkbook in hand
and said, "Brother, you can't fail." When all the
boxing financiers were pulling the rug from
under me with subterfuge and sinister methods,
he came to my rescue.'"

**Daniel's _Pomes_**

"Safari"

The well-known hunter, Mr. Glenn,
Has heads of Kudu hanging in his den,
But the only thing he ever killed with a bullet
Was a pullet.

*Tocqueville on Montalembert:* "A touch of fear tempered his natural insolence and put limits on his perverse and combative vein, for, like many other men of words, he had much greater boldness of language, than stoutness of heart."

## A Visit to the Mumfords

*Lewis and Sophia, Amenia, N.Y.*: Drove down with David Staines. Arrived about 11:00, chatted, had lunch, more talk, & departure. Both Ms showing their age. LM on eve of his 81st birthday, still very much the proud talkative gentleman, concerned about his fame and appearing modestly immodest, or maybe the other way around. Talked a good deal about his youth in NYC and years at CCNY. Sophia's years on the *Dial* came up. She had known Bourne, Veblen, and many others.

One gets the impression that they feel pretty isolated and welcome outside company. Sophia's legs give her pain. She can't take walks, and even walking around the house and standing up to cook are difficult for her. Both excellent hosts, kindly and cheerful. LM tries to be fair & magnanimous, but the resentments he feels towards old enemies or opponents (Edmund Wilson, for example) are close to the surface.

## Van Quine

*Nov. 28*: Long trek with Van and Joe Kaplan.
We took the subway to Quincy & proceeded via
causeways and crossings. Crossed a long bridge.
All the life on the water—ducks, gulls, small
birds—of interest on this warm and tranquil day.
The excursion up & back was about 14 miles.
I ended up with blistered soles thanks to my
ill-fitting shoes. Some lovely views & photo-
graphical sites. Old fortifications probably dating
back to World War I. Van talkative and reminis-
cent—his student days in Oberlin, his graduate
work with Whitehead at Harvard, subsequent
meetings and correspondence with Russell, his
travels all over the world, his interest in languages. Joe did a great deal of listening for he's
now writing about Whitman's New Orleans trip
and fascinated by Quine's travel account.

## Edna Millay's Correspondence

*Edmund Wilson to Floyd Dell:* "This correspondence is full of mysteries, and they will never be cleared up unless they who knew her well leave some testimony. It is not merely a question of gratifying curiosity about somebody's private affairs. The letters and records of writers of genius are one of the only ways we have of finding out how life was really lived in any given time or place."

## Cardinal Newman's Prayer

"O Lord, support us all the day long, until the shadows lengthen and the evening comes, and the busy world is hushed, and the fever of life is over, and our work is done. Then in thy mercy, grant us a safe lodging, and a holy rest, and peace at the last."

## Half Life

It was Bismarck who at 70 remarked to someone
that he didn't think the second half of his life
would be as interesting as the first half.

## Daniel's Dictionary

*Caducity*: (Lat. *caducus*: inclined or ready to fail) (1) frailty of old age, senility. (2) Perishability, impermanence. Hence *caducious*: shedding at certain stages of development.

## Maecenas on Malady

Though racked with gout in hand and foot,
Though cancer deep should strike its root,
Though palsy shake my feeble thighs,
Though hideous lump on shoulder rise,
From flaccid gum teeth drop away,
Yet all is well if life but stay.

## Maturity

*Ortega y Gasset*: "It takes us thirty years at most to recognize the limits within which our possibilities are going to move. We have taken possession of the real, which is like having measured the meters of a chain attached to our feet. Then we say: 'Is this what life is? Nothing more than this? A closed cycle that repeats itself, always identical?' Here is a dangerous hour for every man."

**From the List of Available Occupations Listed by U.S. Census**

"[G]runt men, pullup girl, wet-end operator, snout puller, bladder blower, end fixer, loin puller, dinkey skinner, bung dropper, skull chopper, kibble fixer, fish smeller, clinker cooler, end crotchpiece boaster."

## Daniel's Dictionary

*Libitina*: Roman goddess of corpses & funerals once associated with voluptuary delights, Love/Death.

*Libitinarius*: head undertaker.

*Hearse*: (from Fr. *herse*, Lat. *hirpex*) rake or harrow. A stationary framework of wood to hold the lighted taper placed on a bier or coffin. Looked like a large rectangle rake lying with prongs upward.

*Casket*: around middle of 19th c. substituted for "coffin." Connotes a chest to contain something precious. Less fearful-sounding than "coffin."

"And then—and then it is Chloe, in the dark, stark awake, and Strephon snoring unheeding; or *vice versa*, 'tis poor Strephon that has married a heartless jilt, and awoke out of that absurd vision of conjugal felicity, which was to last for ever, and is over like any other dream."

"I think women have an instinct of dissimulation; they know by nature how to disguise their emotions far better than the most consummate male courtiers can do. Is not the better part of the life of many of them spent in hiding their feelings, in cajoling their tyrants, in masking over with fond smiles and artful gaiety their doubt, or their grief, or their terror?"

**Story Idea:**
**"The Secret Life of Ralph Waldo Emerson"**

Springs from a conversation with Joel Porte. Joel recently discovered that the house or building in which he now has an apartment was originally a resort on Fresh Pond built at the end of the 18th century. It was moved some time in the next century and covered with a ghastly stucco.

The hero of my story is a young scholar who is going through a randy period. Just divorced, he's writing a book on RWE while carrying on with various women. He doesn't make much headway on the book until he learns about the origins of his dwelling and comes across some cryptic passages in Emerson's journal about Margaret Fuller. He concludes that their relationship must have been much closer than he had thought, that in fact, it might have been sexual.

Soon he is dreaming odd dreams. He hears sounds of "transports" in his room. In Widener Library he finds clues he'd missed before, and thanks to his new insights and suspicions, he makes important discoveries about RWE's secret life and overturns the conventional view of a denatured sage with no balls at all. *Au contraire*, Joel's Emerson is a passionate sensual man (hence his excitement at discovering Whitman) and his crisis (circa 1850) had less to do with the Fugitive Slave Law than it did with the drowning of Margaret Fuller and the sense of his failing sexual powers. My story ends with the hero writing madly away, his own appetites having declined to the point where he finds women repulsive and is ever more dependent on the ideas and insights he gained from the nocturnal revelations.

## Dream Couplets: July 20, 1977

Inside that last receptacle of hope
I found what I was looking for—a rope
Which, casually coiled around my upthrust neck,
Made me resemble what I was—a wreck.

## Death of Robert Lowell

*Sept. 13*: I met Lowell in 1934 when he came to 22 Trowbridge where I shared a room with John Finch. He'd come to visit J. V. Healy, the deaf poet and critic and secretary to Boston Mayor James Curley. Lowell at that time was in his last year at Kenyon College. I don't remember very much about him then except that he was Hamlet-ish, aloof. The last time I saw him was in the spring of this year when he came to dinner at 15 Hilliard. He had stopped me and suggested dinner, so I'd asked him to come to our house. He was very gentle and courtly, paid particular attention to Janet, drank a great deal, and seemed to enjoy himself. I can't remember what we talked about, but it wasn't about "literature" or what Janet called "academic."

A half-dozen years ago I bumped into him in Earls Court, London, each of us balancing packages and looking as if we were engaged in some kind of illicit enterprise. I liked him very much. He was a good man.

## Idea for a Utopia

The World as Opera, the singers international
& interracial: a merging of comedy & tragedy.
Harmony. Music & mathematics make the world
kin. Individualism (solos) and choruses (multi-
tudes). The composer is King.

**Story Idea:**
**Caliban of Soldiers Field: "A Tale of Cambridge"**

Plot: A wicked magician, his magic depleted over the centuries, chooses Cambridge—seat of Harvard and MIT—to replenish it. He still has great powers but insufficient to put himself in command of the science resources of the two great centers of learning. However, his agents (gnomes whose minds he has ensnared by his malicious arts and who appear to be ordinary citizens) discover through diligent inquiry that a great atomic center is being constructed under Soldiers Field. He plans to take it over and divert its great machine to achieve his aim: first to take over Cambridge, then Massachusetts, New England, the USA, and finally the World. With his new powers he will foment international wars and reduce the world population to a manageable size.

But unbeknownst to him (and to Cambridge & Harvard as well), a strange half-mad man (call him Caliban) has established himself in the environs of Soldiers Field—Caliban, a sulky woodchuck, angrily muttering to himself, cursing anyone he happens to meet in the dark & early mornings. Boy & Girl, the two other main characters, like to play in Soldiers Field and sometimes encounter him. They're frightened at first but soon they grow used to him and are delighted by his gruffness and angry shouts. They are orphans. They live nearby in an abandoned garage housing old automobiles and racing sculls. Only Caliban knows their secret, although they don't know that he does.

The magician now moves in. He and his gnomes have seized the underground laboratory and work unobserved, because the magician has befogged the minds of the workers and staff. But suddenly he senses that his plot is known to somebody else. But to whom? To someone who has observed the whole operation, constructed a number of secret tunnels and passageways. The magician doesn't even know of Caliban's existence, but at last discovers the children and is about to turn them into crows when Caliban alerts them and hides them in one of his secret burrows. Together they drive the magician and his gnomes crazy.

The magician's power weakens, and the workers and staff revert to their former condition as President Bok of Harvard leads a troop of picked faculty into the underground lab and seizes the culprits. The children receive 4-year scholarships and Caliban is made chief Groundsman.

**Daniel's Dictionary**

*Femtometer*: one quadrillionth of a meter.
"The amoeba marched several femtometers
before it tired."

## To Err Is . . . Strategic

*Oct.* 20: North Korea announces defection of South Korean pilot who flew his light plane across the border. Not a "defection," replies South Korea, but a "navigational error." Very appealing. We don't "sin"—we "err" and make "navigational errors."

## The Puritans

John Robinson's description of unregenerate
England—"the great retchless rout of wicked and
graceless persons." John Winthrop's summation
of England: "coldness, carnality, and contention."
Richard Mather: "Do you think that God liveth
on goat's bloud?"

### High Jinks

From undated letter to Edmund Wilson, possibly suggested by Otis Ferguson's limerick "There was a young man from Belgrave":

Said a widow whose singular vice
Was to keep her dead lover on ice:
"He's so hard now I've lost him
I'll never defrost him,
Cold comfort—but cheap at the price."

## William Blake *Redivivus*

A composition by John Cage
Puts some music lovers "in a rage."

"I didn't run *for* office. I ran *from* office." Does that suggest that at bottom I'm an *office-flee-er*, not an *office-seeker*? One could carry this idea further: "He suffocated under a heap of honors."

## The Underside

The running of concentration camps, fake
trials, torture, etc. usually entrusted to a special
class, putative criminals given license by the
"Authorities." Speaks well for the tenderness
and sensitiveness of the majority of us—right,
left, center—who can't bear to perform these
abominations and are forced to relegate them
to the criminal police. The Over and Under
worlds enjoy an uneasy alliance.

## Some Clerihews in Edmund Wilson's Correspondence

Said Jane Austen to Harry Levin,
"We speak well of you in Heaven."
"We think well of you in Boston,"
Said Harry Levin to Jane Austen.

Said Lionel Trilling to his wife,
"Lawrence hymns the joyous life."
"We are solemn—but we're willing,"
Said his wife to Lionel Trilling.

## Waldo Frank

Often wise, sometimes brilliant, on occasion
the self-appointed pontificating seer, and
utterly humorless—was fond of "rare" words
like "vinculate" (to bind).

## Blind Spots

*Alfred Stieglitz:* "Everyone has his blind spot and until one knows what one's blind spot is, anything that one has to say about oneself must be meaningless . . ."

"It seems never to occur to anyone to go into himself; to question himself. Automatically the other person is wrong. To grow more tolerant towards others, stricter with oneself, seems unheard of. Freedom for all, tolerance towards none, seems to be the slogan."

## Ironic Praise

*Max Beerbohm in* Vanity Fair *(1928)*: "'To the really vain person (especially if he be also really modest) ironic praise is better than no praise at all. I remember my brother Herbert once said, 'I can stand any amount of flattery—if it's only fulsome enough.' And I replied, 'Oh, I make no conditions of any sort.'"

**Story Idea:**
**Plot for Cambridge Series Called *Tales for Children***

An emeritus Professor owns an ancient Raleigh bicycle purchased at the end of World War II. It is still functioning a decade later—but barely. Parts are hard to find. The fenders are beginning to bend and twist. He takes the bike to the repair shop and is advised not to spend his money trying to fix it (by the way, the Professor happens to be an atheist). He feels sad about the bike, which is now positively dangerous to ride. He's really depressed, takes it personally. The dying bicycle signifies the end of himself and his world.

One night, moved by some strange impulse, he descends into the basement of his house to inspect the injured bike and finds it miraculously restored, glitteringly healed, metal fatigue gone. Overjoyed, he takes the bike out. As he turns the pedals, perfume sprays out of the bell on the handlebar and music (hold music) from the brake. Shaken, the Professor stops at a pub on Massachusetts Avenue for a drink. A thief hops on the unwatched bike—but lo! the bike cries out: "Stop this thief! He's stealing the property of my Master!" Clearly a miracle. A policeman apprehends the thief just as the old Professor (who has heard the call and hurried to the rescue) arrives. Now he realizes that he has been wrong about religion, that the bike is a sacred bike and ripe for canonization. People come to his house to pray to the bike, which performs some modest miracles—nothing astonishing but sound cures. The Professor dies content. He knows that the bike will be enshrined in the Bow Street church.

## Suffering

*Henry James to Charles Eliot Norton*: "The human soul is mighty, and it seems to me we hardly know what it may achieve (as well as suffer) until it has been plunged deep into trouble. Then indeed, there seems something infinite in pain and it opens out before us, door within door, and we seem doomed to tread its whole infinitude; but there seems also something infinite in effort and something supremely strong by its own right in the grim residuum of conscious manhood with which we stand face to face to the hard realities of things."

### Re: Alfred Kazin's *New York Jew*

Alfred's autobiography-cum-novel enmeshes
the author in ways he doesn't seem able to
comprehend. It is a dream, a fantasy in which
the dazzling and ubiquitous artist—the friend
of the great, God's spy, the magnetic lover whom
women struggle to keep their hands off—is an
unmitigated success. But at the same time, it's
a canard against the author whose faults are
varnished over with self-esteem. His values are
the decent ones. He can be very penetrating in
his judgments of books, men, institutions. What
he chiefly lacks is *irony*, especially in regard to
*himself*, and *humor*. One of his favorite words is
"hilarious" but his hilarity is usually forced and
unfunny. He's a chronic complainer, a kind of
petty Job who, from time to time, complains to
God that He betrayed him. AK is also betrayed
by false friends who don't rejoice sufficiently
when good fortune befalls him or who aren't
sufficiently remorseful when AK is in the dumps.

All the same, what a fine writer and critic he can
be: perceptive, intelligent, witty.

### Bowerbird

"Any of family *Ptilonorhynchidae* native to
Australia and New Guinea. Males of the species
build bowers out of grasses, twigs, and 'colored
materials' to attract females."

(DA, are you a bowerbird? If not, a related
species?)

## The Unmanured Soul

*George Dalgarno (1623?–1687)*: "But learned worthies, you are of the number of those who have fortunately passed the pillar of ignorance erected in the straits of knowledge, and have given an evident demonstration, that there is yet a vast *America* of unmanured faculties of the soule."

## A Thought

One must act as if one were free. No freedoms
without restraints.

### Daniel's Dictionary

*Scruple*: (from Lat. *scrupus*: a small stone) pebble or small sharp stone. Samuel Johnson prayed to be free of "scruples."

*Emolument*: (from Lat. *molere*: to grind) pay for service rendered, viz., for something "ground out."

*Emolumentum*: a fee for grinding grain.

## Jacques Prévert's "Pater Noster"

Our father who art in heaven
Stay there
And we will stay on earth
Which is at times so lovely
With its mysteries of New York
With its mysteries of Paris
Which absolutely outweigh
   the mystery of the Trinity.

## Text for the J. D. Rockefeller Funeral Sermon

"Thou anointest my head with oil." (Psalm 23)

## If Friendship Means Dependency

God has no friends.

## The Dark Side

In his Samuel Johnson biography, Jack Bate
quotes Edmond Malone to the effect that writers
of others' lives must show the dark sides of their
subjects' (especially heroes and sacred writers)
lives in order to keep mankind from despair.

## Complaints of the Well-to-Do

*Mrs. Thrale Quoting Samuel Johnson*: "It is so *very* difficult for a sick man not to be a scoundrel." He thought that the complaints of the well-to-do were "grossly exaggerated by self-centeredness filling the vacuum of boredom and idleness."

## "Almost every man has some need"

says Johnson, "or imaginary connection with a
celebrated character . . ."

**Marvell, "Bermudas"**

He hangs in shades the Orange bright,
Like golden Lamps in a Green Night.

## Jews with Money

Last night, 7 April, galloped through Joseph
Heller's *Good as Gold* and won't look at it again.
The bent toward self-parody never stronger,
the joke for the joke's sake, the brashness and
calculated outrageousness all pure Heller. More
interesting, I think, is his obsession with Jewishness—his own and his culture's. This is an
"in-Jewish" book full of jokes for Jews, a smirk-
ing conspirational book for insiders—clannish,
steeped in self-hatred and elaborate fantasies
about the blonde, icy, ruthless gentile world (the
equivalent of Black fantasies of the White world).
Laced with self-contempt, is it also an exorciz-
ing, I wonder, of his own dreams and ambitions?
Kissinger is his chief target, his symbol of the
Jew elevated into the world of money and power.
One might argue that Heller's Kissinger is a false
Jew, a renegade, and yet one with whom he and
many Jews can identify.

Finally, after joking about Jews and Jewishness,
he makes peace with the Family. He concludes
that they have always accepted him—the outsider,
the professor—been proud of him in their fierce,
hectoring, "gutsy" way. In the Jewish community—
for all of its vulgarity and harshness—he finds
love and security. In short, the novel is welded in

chunks: an "empty-your-bureau-drawer-novel" into which Heller piled his accumulated resentments, bright cracks, and anxieties.

## Chance Encounters

*William James*: "Their orbits come out of space and lay themselves for a short time along ours, and then off they whirl again into the unknown, leaving us with little more than an impression of their reality and a feeling of baffled curiosity as to the mystery of the beginning and end of their being."

**Daniel's Dictionary**

*Doughboy*: infantryman in World War I. (Origin obscure, but definition: bread dough that is thin and is cut into various shapes is a good characterization of an army of soldiers.)

## Georg Christoph Lichtenberg on the Basics

*On Magnanimity*: ". . . a man is magnanimous rather for the sake of showing off than out of goodness of heart. Those who have it in their nature rarely perceive that it is anything special to be magnanimous."

*On Observations*: "I am convinced that we not only love ourselves in others, but hate ourselves in others too."

"I know that look of affected attentiveness: it is the lowest point of distraction."

"What astonished him was that cats should have two holes cut in their coats exactly at the places where their eyes were."

*On Melancholia*: "Some maladies are so great that we die of them; others, though not exactly mortal, are such as may be observed and felt without much study; finally, there are some that are hardly recognizable without a microscope. But then they look perfectly awful. This microscope is—hypochondria. I believe that if men were really to set themselves to study these microscopical diseases, they would have the satisfaction of being ill every day of their lives."

*On Women & Shame*: "Do people blush for shame in the dark? That people get pale with fright in the dark, I think probable, but not red with shame. For they pale on their own account, but red on account of others as well as themselves. The next question, whether women blush in the dark, is an extremely difficult one; at least it is one on which little light can be thrown."

*On Thinking & Reading*: "Is reading the same as study? It has been stated with much truth and reason that while printing did, indeed, make learning more general, it at the same time diminished its content. Excessive reading is bad for thinking. The most distinguished thinkers I have ever met have been just those of my learned acquaintance who have read the least."

*On Religion & Virtue*: "Might it not be that good men venerate religion, instead of religion making good men; and that they become adherents and defenders of religion because religion teaches their principles?"

*On Old Age & Learning*: "That in advancing years we should grow incapable of learning has some connection with age's intolerance of being ordered about, and a very close connection, too."

*On Sleep*: "Has anyone, I wonder, ever considered sleep as a condition connecting us with plants? History contains accounts exclusively of waking people; but are those of the sleeping less important? True, man does not do much in that condition, but it is precisely there that the wakeful psychologist should have most to do."

*On Divine Service*: "The term 'divine service' ought to be applied no longer to church-going but exclusively to good deeds."

*On Self-knowledge*: "By strictly attending to our thoughts and feelings, and by expressing them so that through a careful choice of promptly-noted words they shall obtain a strongly individual character, we may very quickly lay in a stock of observations in many ways profitable. It makes us acquainted with ourselves for one thing, and lends solidarity and unity to our system of thought . . . Vigilance, practice, and economy with one's thoughts may in the same way be made to compensate for a lack of genius."

*On Concealment*: "Every man also has his moral backside which he refrains from showing unless he has to and keeps covered as long as possible with the trousers of decorum."

*On the Classics*: "The older one grows (presuming one grows wiser with age) the more one loses the hope of being able to write better than the authors of antiquity; in the end one sees that the standard for all that is right and beautiful is nature and that we all bear this gauge within us but so rusted over with prejudices, with words that lack meaning, with false conceptions, that it no longer serves to gauge anything with."

*On Swallowed Knowledge*: "An increase in knowledge acquired too quickly and with too little participation on one's own part is not very fruitful: erudition can produce foliage without bearing fruit."

*On Conversion*: "The conversion of malefactors before their execution can be compared with a species of fattening: they are made spiritually fat and then have their heads cut off so that they shall not lapse again."

*On Causation in History*: "What I dislike in the method of testing history is that people see purpose in every action and trace every event to some intention or other. That is assuredly all wrong. The greatest events come to pass without any design; chance makes blunders good and amplifies the most cleverly laid scheme. The important events in the world are not deliberately brought about; they occur."

## Bad Writers

Bad writers are mostly those who try to express their own feeble ideas in the language of good ones. If they could only say what they think in appropriate words, they would always contribute something towards the common fund, and deserve attention.

"Certain Fat People"

Not at all weighed down by poundage,
Brave and ebullient like balloons in the wind,
They sail down avenues,
Breasting skinny crowds,
Pushing preeminent bellies.

### A Harvard Scene

The look of studied unconcern on the face of
the bearded man in the Yard as his amiable old
mongrel squats on the leaf-strewn grass.

## The Approaching Election

Last night listened to five Republican candidates make their pitch to the Iowa voters. John Anderson of Illinois the only honest and candid one of the lot. The others—smooth, huckstering, unctuous. One of the questions posed to them was whether or not they still believed in America. That brought forth a gush of guff. We've been living in a "crisis situation" for the last two months, touched off by the Iranian revolution and the seizure of American diplomats in Teheran. Then the Russian invasion of Afghanistan, the symptoms of world disorder, and upheaval produced by forces whose origins lay deeper than anyone can even guess. Hints of a coming war—although that prospect at the moment seems remote. The coming year will be a hard one.

## Daniel's Dictionary

*Tossah*: an undomesticated Asian silkworm.
(Good name for one of Dr. Fu Manchu's *femme-fatale* agents.)

*Tumbadero*: (Spanish-Cuban) a punishment area
on an estate. Another word for "World" governed
by God, the Task-Master.

## Daniel Aaron's Death

*Feb. 17*: Last night a dream that would have terrified the Ancients. Sitting around a table with friends—how old or new I can't say. Someone handed me a card with my picture on it. The card announced that Daniel Aaron is dead, one of four killed in a bomb attack. The incident was described in some detail although I can't remember what was written. I had two impulses— deny the report or (more powerful) concede that I was indeed dead, although unaware of my new state until that moment. Life drains away as I say good-bye to my friends. Dismay. The party breaks up.

## Hurricane Names

Current milquetoast samples like Allen, Bonnie, David, Connie? No! Hurricanes deserve names commensurate with their elemental power. Not "Allen" but "Ahab," that violent king who came to a bad end (dogs lapped his blood), or Erebos (son of Chaos and god of Hell), Ragnarok, Thor, Grendel, Goliath, Tamerlane, Dracula, Hitler.

## The Other Vanity Fair

*Becky Sharp*: "But she had the dismal precocity of poverty."

Every day should be a Jewish holiday.
How swiftly the uncrowded buses
Move between predestinated stops.
Unleashed taxis course through crosstown streets.
Policemen doze by pairs in tired squad cars.
The worried city, not quite socked out, naps—
Undisturbed by sobbing synagogues.

### Self-admonition

Old people forget what they ought to remember
and remember too much what they ought to
forget. Watch it!

## Story Idea: The Dope Fiend

A dope fiend attacks & murders the wife of
the President of the United States. "Kill! Kill!"
shouts the mob. No. Justice must be carried out.
The trial. Defendant declared not guilty by virtue
of insanity and is remanded to St. Elizabeth's
Hospital. There he discovers a cure for cancer.

## Prudentius on Forbearance

"Even to Spirits that often do evil
Hell hath its holidays frequently coming;
Languid the torment and milder the punishment."

### Daniel's Dictionary

*Coprolites*: fossil excrement. So we might refer to the "Protocols of Zion" as coprolitic?

*Nematocysts*: stinging cells. (Some critics are armed with such cells.)

## Richard Wilbur's Clerihews for DA's 70th Birthday

Dan
Has completed his Biblical span,
But we'll hope to see him again
For another threescore and ten.

Dan
Fights inflation as well as he can
By intoning such militant chants
As "Ten Cents a Dance!"

Dan
Is not an orangutan.
Still, he always says, "Hi, Mate"
To any higher primate.

Dan
If he walked to Afghanistan,
Would no doubt limp and hobble
As he entered Kabul.

Dan
Attributes his long life to bran.
Also to Moxie, ginseng, Baby Ruth,
And the endless pursuit of Truth.

Dan
Denies that he's Peter Pan,

But his habit of flying about
Leaves observers in doubt.

Dan
Has a racquet that's strung with rattan.
As he wields it he cries, "Take that!
'Ratta-tat-tat!'"

Dan
Disapproves of the Ku Klux Klan.
Their politics just aren't his bag,
And he doesn't like chaps in drag.

Dan
Is a pious and prayerful man.
He was once heard entreating, "*Say*, God,
'How's about an American *Pléiade?*'"

*April 9*: Dinner at Bill Doering's. LH now half-blind and plagued to death with emphysema. Walking with human guidance and support of one of those splayed, three-pronged hospital canes. Bill says she likes me but thinks I don't like her. I met her a few times, which she probably doesn't remember. (I was doing research on *Writers on the Left* and she was very defensive of her Party friends and scornful of the renegades.) Later I saw her at the Wilsons' (she was devoted to Elena), and last at the Morgan Library too. Now close to Dick Poirier, whom she regards as one of her most reliable friends and the finest man she knows, the only one to whom she entrusts her first drafts—because she knows he will be honest.

Bent, haggard, constantly coughing, she was still very far from pitiful. Very spirited and funny, a fine raconteur, and not mean or malicious toward people she hates or hated. Most interesting to me were her comments on Aline Bernstein and Thomas Wolfe. She took a class with Wolfe and remembers him as physically dangerous. During rehearsals of one of LH's plays, Aline would sit next to her and tell her all the ghastly stories of TW's gauche and brutal behavior, his outbursts

("Come out you dirty Jew, and fuck," he would shout as he walked along the corridor outside her room). LH told Aline to stop telling her these stories, that Aline was more disgusting than TW in accepting this behavior.

In her late years LH more beautiful, oddly enough, than she was 20 years ago. Face caved in but redeemed by a powerful nose. Obviously fearful of what's impending. Bill doesn't think she'll last the year. He treats her tenderly and lovingly, and she melts. She keeps thanking everyone for lighting her cigarettes, opening her purse, helping her walk. A proud arrogant woman humiliated by her condition, not ready for death, still tart and funny, her remarks jetting out like gusts from embers.

### "Dopey" Comatosa

A character in DA's unwritten novel of the
New York City underworld—a moribund *capo*
in Cosa Nostra.

## The Carlyles

*Elizabeth Hardwick*: "It all seems negligible, out of proportion, one of those trivial points upon which marital rages ponderously come to rest. Still, the angers and quarrels darkened their lives. The sadness is that, even with a clever and uniquely attractive woman like Jane Carlyle, a conviction of having sacrificed only to be under-valued drove her to despair and pulled Carlyle along with her."

"When Jane Carlyle was cleaning and sweeping and keeping the accounts within discreet limits she certainly did not set a price upon her actions. But, of course, there was a hidden price. It was that in exchange for her work, her dedication, her special if somewhat satirical charms, Carlyle would, as an instance, not go out to Lady Ash-burton when she would rather he stayed at home. This is the unspoken contract of a wife and her works. In the long run wives are to be paid in a peculiar coin—consideration for their feelings. And it usually turns out this is an enormous, unthinkable inflation few men will remit, or if they will, only with a sense of being overcharged."

Nothing I've read deals with this important
subject. The impulse to throw away is invariably
checked by a counter-impulse—to retain—
especially junk (viz., physical or spiritual correl-
atives of *moments* only grudgingly displaced).
My office is glutted with discardable objects.
The time is not far off when I'll consign them
to the trash basket.

## Music Reminders

Well, at last, the key and Köchel number of a Mozart quartet which I still know almost by heart but which I haven't heard for almost ten years. That was in Germany. I listened to it again and again. So here it is: get it. (D minor, K 421, Deutsche Grammophon 2740 249. And add Jan Zelenka's lovely Trio Sonata, No. 6 in C minor.)

## What Do I Believe In?

I believe in Chance, Fortune, Coincidence,
Accident.

## Saccade

An "anticipatory leap" to meet a moving object
(say, a speeding baseball) too fast for the eye to
follow. Now imagine an argument in which one
is being virtually overwhelmed by the speed
of an opponent's verbal discharges. He makes a
"saccade" to another position where he can better
anticipate a lethal assault, adjust himself, and
meet it when it strikes.

**Pay Attention**

One day Elpenor fell off Circe's roof and broke his
neck. DA crashed his bike on Mt. Auburn St.—
a hint from Him.

## The Shah's Widow

*June* 30: Bike ride with Massud Farzan. Told me
about his visit to Her Serene Majesty living opu-
lently on Beekman Place and in her Connecticut
house. The New York apartment swelling with
formidable bodyguards. She is one of Massud's
admirers. Talked to her frankly about his views
on the Shah. Very regal she was, he says, and
beautifully dressed, but also very sad, smoked
incessantly, and (her most unqueenly act) cracked
the joints of her fingers as she conversed. How
about this for an opening sentence? "Ensconced
in opulence, the large-eyed queen chain-smoked
and cracked her knuckles."

## Bulgakov

Mandelstam presaged that, in the future, the novel would be concerned with "the history of the disintegration of biography as a form of personal experience, and even more than disintegration—the catastrophic destruction of biography."

Could this apply, at least to a degree, to Henry Adams' *Education*? For him, as well as for displaced Russian writers (1917–22), the stable world had disintegrated. Adams, like Bulgakov, played down or omitted his successes and underscored his failures.

Bulgakov's *The White Guard*: cp. Hemingway's "Code." Facing impossible situations, the last resort is to behave well. Don't change your convictions (moral or intellectual) "to fit the latest political demand."

Is there a book on "Bureaucracy and the Literary Imagination?" (Suggested authors: Dostoyevsky, Kafka, Musil, Bulgakov, Melville, Nathanael West.)

*D.H. Lawrence*: "The best and most permanent changes are those due to amelioration of manners and morals and not to any violent upheavals."

## Alabama Yankees

"During the late 1940's, Mr. Delmar captivated 20 million radio listeners every Saturday night with his burlesque of a bombastic, super-chauvinistic legislator who drank only from Dixie cups and refused to drive through the Lincoln Tunnel."

His stock expression, "That's a joke, son," was for many years one of the nation's pet phrases, mimicked by children and businessmen alike.

His first introduction, on Oct. 7, 1946, as a member of the Fred Allen gallery, "Allen's Alley," was typical:

> *Allen*: Senator Claghorn . . .
> *Claghorn*: (interrupts) Ah'm from the South. From the deep South!
> *Allen*: From way down South?
> *Claghorn*: Ah'm from so far down South that mah family is treadin' water in the Gulf Stream.
> *Allen*: Gee, that's south, isn't it?
> *Claghorn*: Where I live we call the people from Alabama Yankees.

## Idleness

*William Faulkner:* "I found out some time back that it's idleness breeds all our virtues, our most bearable qualities—contemplation, equableness, laziness, letting other people alone; good digestion mental and physical; the wisdom to concentrate on fleshly pleasures—eating and evacuating and fornication and sitting in the sun . . ."

## Time

*Emerson*: "Time dissipates to shining ether the
solid angularity of facts."

## Sunrise

*Sept.* 23: Up at 6:30. Run 12 laps of a quarter-mile track. The sun a huge swollen red globe hanging low on the Boston skyline.

   After a rough night,
   The choleric sun
   Rises red,
   Showers and shaves
   And steps out white with light.

## New Scholarship

Oh, my dear!
Shocking news, I fear.
The Queen of Calvary got laid!
From incest Hawthorne's guilt was made!

## Fond of Reading

*Gertrude Stein to Edmund Wilson in Response to His Piece on Her in* Vanity Fair, *Oct. 3, 1923:* "I am awfully pleased with it, awfully awfully pleased with it. I don't believe you do me more than justice but you do me a whole lot of justice . . . all literature is to me me, that isn't as bad as it sounds. Some one complained that I always stopped while I was driving to read the sign posts even when I knew the road and all I could explain was that I am fond of reading . . ."

**Daniel's Dictionary**

*Scaturience*: (rare, Scottish origin) a gushing forth, an effusion, "a shimmering scaturience of an intelligence and sensibility." Edmund Wilson used it in his review of E.E. Cummings' *Him*.

## A Recollection of Henry James

A son of William James writes to Edmund Wilson
re: Henry James the novelist. An incident about
HJ and one of the Emmet girl cousins who asked
for more "chikn." "My dear Leslie, don't say
chikn, say chick-en." "Oh, cousin Henry, you're
crool!" "Not 'crool' but 'cruel.'" "Well, I think
I will go upstairs and fix my hair." "My dear Leslie,
fix it *to* what and *with* what?"

## Addled Adulation

*Robert Lowell to Edmund Wilson re: JFK's White
House Party for Writers and Intellectuals, May 13,
1962:* "Except for you, everyone there seemed
addled with adulation at having been invited. It
was all good fun but next morning you read that
the President has sent the 7th fleet to Laos, or he
might have invaded Cuba again—not that he will,
but I feel we intellectuals play a very pompous
and frivolous role—we should be windows, not
window-dressing. Then, now in our times, of all
times, the sword hangs over us and our children,
and not a voice is lifted. I thought of all the big
names there, only you acted like yourself."

## The Lost Tribe

*Margaret Marshall to Edmund Wilson, Jan. 9, 1953:*
There would be no problem getting her autobiography published, she tells him, if she had had
a Jewish childhood. She'd considered a spoof on
Norman Podhoretz: "I started from a point much
lower than his. I was a Mormon: of course, if I'd
had any sense, I would have pretended to be a Jew,
especially after I got to New York, and I could
have at least claimed to be a Jew by association
because the original Mormons were one of the
Lost Tribes of Israel."

writes of being thrown into "a lethargy of excitement." I think Eudora Welty would have liked that phrase.

"Saint Cacophony Day"

What a shudder of organs,
Rattle of drums,
Bleating of flutes.

Silent the mellow cello,
Mournful horn,
Violated viola,

Nothing pianissimo
On this loud unbuttoned day.

## Van Wyck Brooks

*Jan. 17*: Thought on this cold snowy morning,
that I might write an "homage" to Van Wyck
Brooks, fallible author of *The Confident Years*.
I don't think any other critic has read as much
American writing or managed to distill it so
successfully. His *Makers and Finders* (a kind of
"American Literary Annals") is personal, often
(from my point of view) mistaken—such as
his portrayal of Sinclair Lewis as a Midwestern
Whitman—but he has good reason to reject the
denigrations of the academic purists, technicians,
aesthetes, and political doctrinaires. He seeks
to immerse himself in an "American culture"
passed over or smothered. The "American Studies"
crowd ought to be required to read *Makers and
Finders*. His picture should be on the walls of
14 East 60th St. office of the Library of America.

I note on p. 537 of *The Confident Years* one of the
many aperçus that dot his series—the place of the
saloon in American writing and art circa 1890–
1940 (Crane, London, O'Neill, Dreiser, Hemingway, etc.), the era washed in booze, the bar as
confessional. The saloon as Valhalla, the last refuge for the last romantics: Huneker's and Menck-
en's celebration of beer. The "Little Renaissance"
a collective protest against "Prohibitions."

Well, then. Why not a little book of "Homages," a defense of the forgotten, the superannuated, rejected, embalmed—a salvage operation to extract the "saving remnants." Brooks, to repeat, makes America *interesting*. Strange reading him today when the shoddy, the corrupt, the dangerous, the spoiled bulk large. Evangelical, often shrill, sometimes mean in his aspersions—vindictive even—Brooks is always motivated, I think, by a passion to exalt his country. This was true even in his first tart strictures on American "Puritanism," parochialism, dullness. There's not such a break, as many assume, between his sharp carpings and his latter-day "croonings" (*pace* Edmund Wilson). Brooks, always the evangelist.

## Men and Women

*Sherwood Anderson:* "Men who love many women never love one woman."

### Betrayals

*C.S. Peirce*: "It is the belief men betray and not
that which they parade which has to be studied."
(Yes, especially now in these hyena days of Ronald
Reagan, emblem of national bilge.) Still, befouled
values and assumptions pitifully throb.

## Back and Forth

*Kierkegaard*: "Life can only be understood backwards; it can only be lived forwards."

## Art of Description

*Otto Rank*: "To best describe something, think of a person you love and to whom you want to tell it."

## The Beautiful Features

*James Fenimore Cooper*, The Pioneers: "'Really, dear sir,' said Elizabeth, projecting her beautiful underlip."

### Stravinsky's Description of Aging

"The ever-shrinking perimeter of pleasure."

## Triumph of Truth

*Max Planck*: "A new scientific truth does not triumph by convincing its opponents and making them see the light, but rather because its opponents eventually die, and a new generation grows up that is familiar with it."

## Definition of a Computer

*Comment of French Historian:* "A huge supplementary brain within reach of the first imbecile would end up multiplying idiocies."

## Instinct

John Bayley speaks of Yeats' and Eliot's canny "instinct for the Zeitgeist."

**From George Herbert, "The Forerunners"**

"Go birds of spring: let winter have his fee;
Let a bleak paleness chalk the doore,
So all within be livelier than before."

## Daniel's Dictionary

*Fossick*: (1) to search for gold by reworking washings or waste piles. (2) To rummage or search, to bustle about (from "fuss").

## Declarations

"I can't pay" is a more passionate declaration than
"I love you."

## The Ploy

"To catch a crowd, catch a prince."

## Appropriating the Thoughts of Others

*Santayana*: "The most contagious feelings, the clearest thoughts, of others are clear and contagious only because I can readily make them my own. I cannot conceive deeper thoughts than my lead can plumb, nor feelings for which I lack the organ."

*Santayana*: "A free mind does not measure the worth of anything by the worth of anything else."

## Dream

Last night a dream like a Lewis Hines photograph.
I'm standing inside a huge garage-like structure.
Parked outside three vehicles—(1) an old Ford
convertible, the first car I learned to drive. It
was squashed in, battered, ready for demolition,
which presumably awaited it inside the cavern-
ous structure. (2) A huge bus and (3) a 10-ton
truck also consigned to the crusher. What sticks
out in the dream (*pace* the Freudians) is the
blunted front end of the Ford. I felt no anxiety
or distress, although I read the dream as a
premonition of mortality. Another vivid dream
followed, but I can't remember it.

When I was young in Europe,
Beds of women blotted out monuments.
They blossom still in the heart's garden.
(I hear the click of high heels in the corridor.)
Time pricks, memory swells.
Only arteries harden.

## The Predicament

*Santayana*: "Poets and philosophers sometimes talk as if life were an entertainment, a feast of ordered sensations; but the poets, if not the philosophers, know too well in their hearts that life is no such thing: it is a predicament. We are caught in it; it is something compulsory, urgent, dangerous, and tempting. We are surrounded by enormous, mysterious, only half-friendly forces."

## Reminder

Reviewing John Rewald's book on Cézanne, John
Golding notes that so much art history today
emphasizes the psychological, sociological, and
linguistic methodologies that "it is salutary to be
reminded by a book such as this that art is just
as much the product of character and courage,
of the clash and cross-fertilization of personalities as of ideas, of the distillation and sublima-
tion of what is most shadowy and savage in the
human psyche as well as that which is finest and
best." (Cp. Montaigne, Tolstoy, Chekhov.)

## Drug-taking

*Aldous Huxley*: "a chemical vacation from intolerable selfhood."

*Giorgos Seferiadis (Review of His Journals)*:
Problems of artist-poet who is also a civil
servant familiar with customs and traditions
of his country, regarding them dispassionately,
yet tied to politicians "at the mercy of circumstances and unexamined emotions." Another
variation on theme of *Writers and Politics*.
One tack taken by Santayana leads to ineffable
serenity but also to celestial chill—a realm of
"essence" beyond the ravaging passions, idiocies,
brutalities GS surveyed from afar.

Well, I must read Seferis. Is he a larger and more
life-embracing T. S. Eliot, whom he admired so
much? I like his reply to one who accused him
of lacking an ideology. His writing, he replied,
had "crystallized round an organical moral stem."
(Could TSE have said as much? Or Santayana?)
Note the poet's reply to man of power, ignored
like the warnings of the Soothsayer to Caesar.
Men of power will "never be diverted from their
ends." Xerxes again and again. Retribution inevitable for men who forget a maxim of Archbishop
Makriyannis—"the earth has no handles by which
a man can heave it onto his shoulder."

## Dr. Johnson Again

"He who makes a beast of himself gets rid of the pain of being a man."

## Chicken Little's Complaint

Said Chicken Little,
Watching the collapsing sky,
"How unjust it is
That I must die."

## Story Idea: Opening Lines

"My mother warned me that if I wore my
rubbers in the house, I'd get sore eyes."

"How would you like to sleep with a corpse?"
I asked her. "I mean me." She looked at me,
a bit unsteady. "What kind of question is that?"

## Genesis of Masterpieces

"For masterpieces are not single and solitary births," wrote Virginia Woolf. "They are the outcome of many years of thinking in common, of thinking by the body of the people, so that the experience of the mass is behind the single voice."

So Walt Whitman implied: but is it so? According to Gillian Beer, "The desire to give space and meaning to unregarded lives is a political project for Woolf."

## Art and Politics

*Chekhov*: "Major writers and artists should engage in politics only enough to protect themselves from it."

## Art and Leisure

*J. J. Chapman*: "The men and women who make the best boon companions seem to have given up hope of doing something else. They have, perhaps, tried to be poets or painters; they have tried to be actors, scientists and musicians. But some defect of talent or of opportunity has cut them off from their pet ambition and has thus left them with leisure to take an interest in the lives of others. Your ambitious man is selfish. No matter how secret his ambition may be, it makes him keep his thought at home . . . But the heartbroken people,—if I may use the word in a mild benevolent sense—the people whose wills are subdued to fate, give us consideration, recognition and welcome."

**Ed Lahey**

*Mary McGrory,* Boston Globe, *July 20, 1969:*

"In a city of replaceable men, Ed Lahey was irre-
placeable. He was the only one of his kind."

"A lot of people feel wounded and lonely because
he is gone. He kept the Press Corps and Presidents
honest. He was the friend of the down and out."

"He wore loud shirts and canvas shoes and talked
out of the side of his mouth. He was mournful
and funny. He occasionally—deliberately—used
bad grammar and wrote the best copy in town,
slashing to the bone of the complicated or the
inflated."

"As a matter of principle, he boycotted background press conferences and private dinners
with secretaries of state. He joined the Gridiron
Club, one of his rare gestures to the establishment, and always referred to it as 'the College
of Cardinals.'"

"He was out of the 'Front Page' tradition of
Chicago newspapering, and he covered the
government like a police beat. He was so nice
to elevator operators, news vendors, bores and
misfits that he had the reputation of being the

kindest man in Washington. And he was—until he got to the typewriter."

"He gleefully baited the mighty and delighted in telling stories about being put down by waitresses. He thought self-importance, self-pity and self-righteousness were unforgiveable."

"His motto, repeated to young reporters whom he treated with a patience he never showed the powerful, was 'fawn not upon the mighty.' This was a quote from his favorite author, Thomas à Kempis."

"He followed it to the letter. Once he described Lyndon Johnson as a man with a terrible regional inferiority complex 'which showed up like dandruff on a dark blue suit.' Asked by a group of Amherst students why Richard Nixon lost the last election, he replied succinctly: 'Because he looked like an Armenian trying to peddle a hot rug'. . ."

"His friend and colleague I. F. Stone said of him: 'He was a medieval figure, really Irish, a sort of pilgrim who came to the business via the race track and the saloon, registering human suffering on his own homemade flute.'"

## Burial Thought

"Sad is the burying in the sunshine
But bless'd is the corpse that goeth home in rain."

## Equivalents

*Alan Bennett re: Max Brod*: "[He] was spared the fate of equivalent figures in English culture, an endless round of arts programmes where those who have known the famous are publicly debriefed of their memories, knowing as their own dusk falls that they will be remembered only for remembering someone else."

## Francis Parkman's Definition of Democracy

"[O]rganized ignorance, led by unscrupulous craft, and marching, amid the applause of fools, under the flag of equal rights." (See Reagan Administration.)

## "The Eve of St. Agnes" in Kiplingese

St. Hagnes Heve! 'ow bloomin' chill it was!
The Howl, for all his hulster, was a-cold.
The 'are limped tremblin' through the blarsted
      grass
Etc., etc.

## Composers

Relax and have no fear:
Here's Meyerbeer.

I'm at your call and beck,
Leoš Janáček.

When steeped in dull repose,
Play Berlioz.

## Broadside

On trial of Queen Caroline, consort of George IV,
whose attempt to divorce her was rejected by Par-
liament. (Had she lived adulterously with valet?)

Most gracious Queen, we thee implore
To go away and sin no more;
Or, if that effort be too great,
To go away, at any rate.

## Old Age

*Graham Greene*: "A crack in the plaster of a neglected house grows more quickly than a line on a human face, paint changes color more rapidly than hair, and a room's decay is continuous: it never comes to a temporary halt on that high plateau of old age where a man may live a long time without apparent change."

## That's My Girl

*Ad for Victoria Houston's* Loving a Younger Man:
"For women who won't settle for anything less
than complete love and happiness."

## Daniel's Dictionary

*Gralloching*: (Gaelic *grealach*: entrail) the process of disemboweling a deer.

## Terminal

*Santayana*: "There is no cure for birth or death save to enjoy the interval."

## Story Idea: Last Sentence in My Gothic Novel

"The flames embraced him lovingly: he positively glowed."

## Satires of John Oldham

"On the whole, it is when Oldham can move from ideas to human situation that he shifts up a poetic gear, and he has the true satirist's gift of gaining in edge and lucidity as the emotional temperature rises (where the rest of us lose control as we essay damaging invective). Even in the rougher satires of the Jesuits, there are moments of superb scorn, inventive and mouth-filling comminations, almost farcical inventories of corruption:

> Should I tell you all their countless Knaveries,
> Their Cheats, and Shams, and Forgeries, and
>     Lies,
> Their Cringings, Crossings, Censings,
>     Sprinklings, Chrisms,
> Their Conjurings, and Spells and Exorcisms;
> Their motly Habits, Maniples, and Stoles,
> Albs, Ammits, Rochets, Chimers, Hoods and
>     Cowls . . ."

*Feb. 24*: Notice the bland benignant look on the faces of certain older men—a wise-guise (unearned).

### Incongruity

From the comical to grotesque. If I say,
"the piccolo thundered and the tuba trilled,"
I simply employ the humor of reversal, i.e.,
the oxymoron.

### Rondure

Suggests a quality of feminine beauty, "something circular or gently rounded." Contrast to John Cleveland's "straight-limbed geometry" ("Mark Antony") or Robert Herrick's "wild civility."

## Characters for My Children's Stories

"He had blazing blue eyes. I don't say they were
just bright eyes. They actually flashed and blazed
depending on how he felt, what he intended.
I mean, he didn't need a flashlight at night, and
he could open his eyes wide enough to illuminate
a cornfield or narrow enough to focus on a target."
(That would be my version of one of my hero's
protective company. See "Longshanks, Girth, and
Keen.")

Another companion and aide: the Fire-Thrower
or Fire-Spitter who astonishes and terrifies by
emitting jets of flame from his mouth. He can
shoot them 50 yards or more. His brother, the
Water-Spouter, can eject water with the explosive
force of a fire hose.

## Hotels in American Literature

Much written on this subject, little deep or exploratory, yet a correlative to theme of American Loneliness and of much that's special and illuminating in some of the stories of Crane, O. Henry, Dreiser, Anderson. Consider Robert Herrick's reflections on Big City hotels (circa 1900–1913) as barracks or vast caravansaries for businessmen and salesmen, or as temples for pipe dreamers.

## Marriage

*My Thought for the Day, July 17*: Marriages are preserved not so much by mutual love and understanding and respect (which, alas, attenuate) but by the civility of the partners.

## Alligator Rides

Charles Waterton (1782–1865), "the eccentric
Yorkshireman and author of the best zoological
travel book in the language." This must be
*Wanderings in South America* (1825), which
contains a famous description of his ride on
an alligator. Darwin describes a visit to CW
in a letter to Lyell and a dinner party attended
by two Catholic priests "and two mulatresses."
At 60 years, CW ran down and caught a leveret
in a turnip patch.

## Tyranny

"Illness and death are, perhaps, the only things
that a tyrant has in common with his subjects."
Cp. Sir Walter Raleigh who defined tyranny as
"a violent form of government, not respecting
the good of the subject, but only the pleasure
of the Commander."

## Theory

*H. C. Languet-Higgins:* "The trouble with rigorous theories is that they are as easy to demolish as they are difficult to construct, while there is a certain security in the incurable imprecision of ordinary language."

## Execrations

"May your womb remain as dry as mouse-shit in a sack," a line from the libretto of Rimsky-Korsakov's *Christmas Eve*, written by himself.

New York Times, *Jan. 17*: "The healthy heart
dances, while the dying organ can merely march."
(Namely, regularity a sign of decline.)

### Epitaph for Our Time

The vice, the vine, the strangler fig
The fault of thinking small and acting big
Have primed the bomb and pulled the pin
And we're all together when the roof falls in!
—James Fenton, "The Ballad of the Shrieking Man"

**Thought for the Day**

*Jan.* 28: "Everybody is somebody's disappointment."

**—istic**

A Black leader describes a wrong and dangerous tactic as "adventuristic, opportunistic, and Custeristic."

## Protesters and the "Folk"

Tapping tribal founts. How "Folk" can serve reactionary nationalism (Hitler). Radical implications; attack vs. genteel culture; how it is processed by ideology; by media.

Who espouse the "Folk"? The "Folk" itself? No, rather the commercial Middle Class. "Folk" as hoked-up simplicity. Anthropological research, excavations, catalogues, texts a far cry from folk-singing gatherings where young and older gurus come to "protest" vs. pollution, Apartheid, bombs, etc. This is idealism-cum-commerce, a smearing over of gritty realities, a vent for private rages which encourage self-righteousness. Protests against parents, schools, social repression. Folk singers indulge in sarcasm yet are susceptible to satire and parody. Cornerstones of Folk: sincerity, pseudo-simplicity, above all, earnestness. Folk singing and styles of living, fashion, dress, manners. Folk-pop. Folk as Big Business.

## Chance

Every person has a "chance at life." The phrase is
William James'. It should be in the mind of every
biographer and autobiographer. What is that
"Chance," and how did the person or the "I" see
and respond to it? As I approach my 77th year,
I ask myself that question. "Chance"—great word.

## Aspects of Marriage

*Thornton Wilder:* "One has seen these insulted husbands finally withdrawing into themselves; they have learned the basic solitude of man as their happier brothers will never know it."

## The Fog

*London Letter from Henry Adams, Sept. 1863:*
"Yet I am willing to do England the justice to say
that while enjoying equally with all nations the
baseness which is inevitable to politics carried on
as they must be, she still has a conscience, though
it is weak, ineffective, and foggy." (Now substitute "the United States" for "England.")

## Daniel's Dictionary

*Noration*: "loud or prolonged talking, a great noise of clamour; a disturbance, fuss."

*Tettered*: Henry Adams described Jefferson's skin as "tettered," namely "scaled" or "patched" as if by a skin disease, psoriasis.

*Hydrocele*: Gibbon suffered from a "hydrocele," "a pathological accumulation of serous fluid in the scrotal pouch so monstrous that he couldn't sit down."

*Tsunami*: huge tidal wave caused by underwater earthquake. Japanese *tsu* (port, harbor) and *nami* (wave). Thus, "the huge tsunami that wreaked such tsuris on Tsushima ended the threatened thrust of the tsetse-fly."

## Story Idea: Opening Sentence

"Can it really be?" Cecily asked, her untampered eyebrows elevated in interrogation. "I suppose so," replied her companion, whose charming smile revealed a shining molar capped in purest gold, "for I, too, observed it."

## A Model Letter of Recommendation

*Benjamin Franklin, Paris, April 2, 1777*: "Sir:—
The bearer of this, who is going to America,
presses me to give him a Letter of Recommen-
dation, tho' I know nothing of him, not even his
Name. This may seem extraordinary, but I assure
you it is not uncommon here. Sometimes indeed
one unknown Person brings another equally unknown, to recommend him; and sometimes they
recommend one another! As for this Gentleman,
I must refer you to himself for his Character
and Merits, with which he is certainly better
acquainted than I can possibly be. I recommend
him however to those Civilities, which every
Stranger, of whom one knows no harm, has a
Right to; and I request you will do him all the
good Offices, and show him all the Favour that,
on further Acquaintance, you shall find him to
deserve. I have the Honour to be, &c. B.F."

"Senectus"

Old people,
Active or still,
Over or under the hill,
Single-tongued
Or polyglot,
Pee a lot.

**Titles**

"Queen for a Day," by Doris Gudinov.

*The Bride Molester,* by Elder Randyman.

*Now You See Me, Now You Don't,* by Raymond Flasher.

## Regression

*From a Harvard University Report on Owen Flanagan's* Varieties of Moral Personality: "I particularly like the parable of the tunicate, or sea squirt, offered in illustration of the possibility of regression: it transpires that for the tunicate adulthood consists in giving up the wandering ways for which it needed a brain, absorbing its own brain and turning, in effect, into a vegetable."

## A Diplomatic Letter of Thanks

*H.W. Longfellow's Note to Thomas Bailey Aldrich upon Receiving TBA's Volume of Poems, Nov. 28, 1865*: "So much depends upon one's mood of mind in reading poetry as well as in writing it, that I shall not attempt to point out what I like best in the volume, or, at all events, not to say that this is better than that, and award first and second prizes to different poems. That sort of judgment one often has occasion to reverse."

## On the Death of James K. Polk

*Lines Quoted in Longfellow's Journal:*

"And from the world the Christian statesman
    fled
When James K. Polk was numbered with the
    dead."

### Medicine Cabinet

*Whip scorpion* (mastigoproctus giganteus), commonly known as a "vine-gardoon," emits "a carefully aimed defensive spray" that can "readily penetrate cockroach cuticle."

*Semiochemicals* (chemical compounds that carry signals)

*Pheromones* (chemical messengers that carry information)

*Bombykol* (sex attractant of female silk moth, *Bombyx mori*)

*N.B.:* Moths court and mate at night, while butterflies are daytime lovers.

**Roorback**

A slanderous lie told for political purposes. Baron von Roorback, fictional author of an imaginary "Roorback's Tour through the United States" published to disparage candidacy of James K. Polk.

## Warren House Office

My office, my "orifice, cavity, vent," my private
shrine. I'm here before 8 AM. All is orderly, spacious, empty. I sit at a tidy desk. Though untran-
quil inside, I relax in this affable, book-bolstered
bunker of light. I stretch out my arms to the
spirit of this great good place. A Haydn concerto
playing, I say to God, "If you snatch me this very
minute, that's all right. I've had my share."

## The Warrens

*The Mount Vernon Street Warrens*: A family saga
of great interest: old-stock Yankee Samuel Warren, his slightly more "social" wife. Sam makes
the "fortune" by working hard and honorably
and building a paper manufacturing business
into large and lucrative enterprise. (Sam could
have served as a model for W.D. Howells' Silas
Lapham.) Sam's wife a powerful and dominating woman, bore him six children. One died in
infancy, the others developed into five distinct,
not unremarkable types.

Henry Warren bought the Beck House (now
Warren House) in 1883 and willed it to Harvard.
Crippled in infancy after falling out of his baby
carriage (he grew only to 5 feet), Henry lived
pretty much the life of a recluse, befriended by
the Harvard Sanskrit scholar, Charles Lanman.
With Lanman's encouragement, he became the
foremost scholar of Buddhism in the U.S. and an
authority on the Pali language.

Author Martin Green skillfully interweaves the
lives of the siblings Cornelia, Edward (Ned), Sam,
Fiske—one of the most extraordinary collections
of brothers and sisters I've come across. Makings
of a family tragedy early discernible and unerringly

resolved—the key rivals the homosexual Boston-hating Ned (who established his own aesthetic coterie in Oxford) and the manly sporting, fashionable, public-spirited Sam. The former befriends Bernard Berenson; the latter, Louis Brandeis. Ned drives Sam to suicide. The experiments and deeds and books of the others fill out the narrative.

## Francis Parkman

Reading Howard Doughty's fine book on Parkman
and struck by this Puritan-Federalist aristocrat's
high-minded credo: honor, courage, reverence.
He disdains the ruck of men, the base "base" of
the population, the foolish boorish majority. He
is insulated by class and upbringing from the
sprawling, sloppy, warm, venial, relaxed, loose,
inconsistent, untrustworthy, bending common-
ality. I see him as a Yankee Pindar. Shakespeare
appreciated the type, ditto Cervantes, even as
they relished the dirt and splendor of mankind.
And it's easy to see why these lonely Coriolanuses
and elegant sprouts—creatures without disfig-
uring incongruities, disciplined dancers—should
attract artists and poets, for in their way they
are "poems." Parkman's La Salle and some of his
other Great Gentlemen are rare, antique museum
pieces, uncommon men and unsuited for survival.

## Woman to Woman

If beating can reform a wife
   It might reform a husband too,
Since such are the effects of strife—
   My sisters, I advise that you

Should try it, not with fists—Oh no!
   For that would seem like some weak joker,
In husband-curing let each blow
   Be given with the kitchen poker!

## Thought for the Week

*Sept. 12*: Design for a new religion, secular and
transcendental. God equals Music—the only
ecumenical, harmonious, organization of spirit.
Come, all ye nations, races, tribes. Hear and sing
the Universal. Fire and wind and mountains
and oceans, the crash of subterranean plates
reconciled by the arts of men. No vengeful gods
and priests, no Jesus Christ needed, no Moses
or Mohammed nor sleek evangelist. Monteverdi,
Bach, Handel, Haydn, Mozart, Beethoven,
Schubert, Berlioz, etc. the ministering angels.
Through them come messages from Outside.
No denial of chaos, pain, tragedy, evil, suffering,
horrors, and abominations but their distillation
possibilized in a cosmic oratorio of light and joy.
In this new religion, church services are concerts.
All speech is sung. Doctrine is implicit in musical
forms and structures. Musicians constitute the
clergy, acolytes of song and sound. Children are
indoctrinated from infancy with musical mathematics of heavenly spheres. Infinite variety and
enriching differences of cultures sustained by a
primordial appetite that links all the peoples of
the world. Hallelujah!

## Love

Glenway Wescott quotes Sir Thomas Browne
on "that magic realm" of "love" when "two people
'so become one that they both become two.'"
Doesn't last long after "young manhood and
young womanhood."

**Daniel's Dictionary**

*Comesis*: the art of improving and preserving natural beauty.

*Onomastic coincidence*: two people having same name.

*Thrawn*: crooked, perverse: "the thrawn theologies of Huysmans."

## Tactics

General Wisdom divides his armies, one prong
turning back to invest the Kingdom of the Past,
the other pressing toward the misty Kingdom of
the Future. In time, they meet.

**Art**

*Arnold Schoenberg*: "Art is the cry of despair of those who experience in themselves the fate of all mankind."

*June 21*: *The Wolf Man* with Lon Chaney Jr.,
Claude Rains. Bitten by a werewolf, Larry
Talbot grows fangs, fur, and a snout, and
begs his father for help.

## Old Age (in Sum)

(1) A diminishing of kissing, (2) a weaker stream in pissing, (3) a horrible penchant for reminiscing.

## Charles Tomlinson re: Neruda

"The lure of titanism that ever lurks amid
America's vastnesses and vacancies."

Like Neruda, some American poets
"incapable of knowing where to stop."

## Inscription on a Medal

"As Soone. As. We. To. Bee. Begunne: / Wee. Did. Beginne. To. Bee. Undone."

## Re: My 79th birthday

Instinctively, I write 69 before crossing it out and
correcting it. No alarming signs yet of senility or
want of desire. ("Performance" another matter.)
I await the "next day" with impatience and bury
myself like an insect in the nutritious pulp of the
past. Inexhaustible stores of the unseen, unread,
unheard, and untasted. Plenty of evidence of
stupendously global horror but don't want to
poison my remaining hours with unproductive
brooding. Is this wisdom or cowardice? How to
exploit the perquisites of age without becoming
an ass or bore?

## Politics

"The Russians don't know when they're well off,"
growled Gorbachev.

"French policy is always rationally planned,"
said Mitterrand.

"We're near and yet so far,"
cried Pérez de Cuéllar.

"Saddam is weakening! Give him a push,"
urged President Bush.

"Germany has regained its soul,"
announced President Kohl.

"Do you detect anything sinister
About England's Prime Minister?"

**Eusociality**

Phenomena exhibited by wasps, bees, ants, termites "that live in colonies of overlapping generations in which one or a few individuals produce all the offspring and the rest serve as functionally sterile helpers in rearing the young and protecting the colony." Not known until the mid-1970s that eusociality existed in mammals (simple forms, to be sure). The mole-rat lives underground, has the smallest brain "relative to his size, of any group of small animals." Feeds on tubers and its own feces (nutritious) and devours its own young.

### When the Old Man Dies

In poorly educated Muslim communities, the loss of an old person was likened to a library burning down, for knowledge was stored in the elderly.

## The Pathos of the Public Library

*Samuel Johnson*: "No place affords a more striking conviction of the vanity of human hopes, than a publick library; for who can see the wall crouded on every side by mighty volumes, the works of laborious meditation, and accurate enquiry, now scarcely known but by the catalogue, and preserved only to increase the pomp of learning, without considering how many hours have been wasted in vain endeavours, how often imagination has anticipated the praises of futurity, how many statues have risen to the eye of vanity, how many ideal converts have elevated zeal, how often wit has exulted in the eternal infamy of his antagonists, and dogmatism has delighted in the gradual advances of his authority, the immutability of his decrees, and the perpetuity of his power? . . . Of the innumerable authors whose performances are thus treasured up in magnificent obscurity, most are forgotten, because they never deserved to be remembered, and owed the honours which they once obtained, not to judgment or to genius, to labour or to art, but to the prejudice of faction, the stratagem of intrigue, or the servility of adulation."

**Frank Kermode**

"Fame can be aphrodisiac, but old age is normally not, and the latter will normally ensure the transience of any sexual attraction caused by the former."

## The Death of John C. Calhoun

In the mélange of last night's dreams (Nov. 4),
a large and buoyant dog-like bear gamboling on
a green lawn and affectionately lapping my face.
Most dramatic, I watch the death of J.C. Calhoun
on a railway car. He has a stroke or heart attack.
I summon help, but he dies after a bit, his body
slumped on the seat.

## Line

"His ear was so keen he could hear her fingernails growing."

## The New Scholarship

Jim Engell quotes title of a current doctoral
dissertation: "Living on the Hymen: Toward a
Totemic Theory of Female Gothic Positionality."

## Medieval Islamic Opinion of Jesus

*Julie Scott Meisami*: "The most amazing thing in the world is that Christians say that Jesus is divine, that he is God, and that they say the Jews seized him and crucified him. How then can a God who cannot protect himself protect others?"

"Anyone who believes that his God came out of a woman's privates is quite mad."

## Leopardi

"Works of genius have this intrinsic property that
even when they give a perfect likeness of the
nullity of things, even when they clearly demon-
strate and make us feel the inevitable unhap-
piness of life, even when they express the most
terrible despair, nevertheless to a great soul . . .
they always serve as a consolation, rekindling
enthusiasm, and though speaking of and portray-
ing nothing but death, restore to it, at least for a
while, the life that it had lost."

### Dr. Johnson

"I love the acquaintance of young people . . . I love
the young dogs of this age; they have more wit
and humour and knowledge of life than we had;
but then the dogs are not so good scholars."

## Stoicism

*Stefan Collini*: "The conscious adoption of stoicism is always in part an expression of disappointment (without some notion of unsatisfied or unsatisfiable wishes, the renunciatory element in stoicism has no point)."

## Petrarch's Conversation Fragments

"Yes, of course I do, but you presume too much and too quickly."

"Sometimes I think time erodes resentments and guilt, but perhaps it only refines them."

"I do hope that Fortune will never again catch me in tears; I shall stand erect if I can, and if not, she will lay me low, tearless and silent."

*George Orwell*: "In the queerest way, pleasure and disgust are linked together. The human body is beautiful: it is also repulsive and ridiculous, a fact which can be verified at any swimming pool. The sexual organs are objects of desire and loathing, so much so that in many languages, if not in all languages, their names are used as words of abuse."

**Daniel's *Pomes***

November Haiku

Trembling in wet cold,
Leaf-stripped, the naked maple
Silently repines.

## Definition of a Picture

*Edgar Degas*: "A picture is something which calls for as much cunning, trickery and vice as the preparation of a crime."

## Cyborg

*The American Heritage Dictionary*: "a human being who has certain physiological processes aided or controlled by mechanical or electronic devices."

## Heartacher

*Roy Roberts*: "You know darn well that no woman
is going to get in a car with seven heartachers."
(I suppose it means what it sounds like.)

## Revolutions

All revolutions devour their children. In turn they are devoured by history, digested, and excreted. They temporarily add a few calories to history—give it a push, fatten it up, or poison it—but not for very long. (My gloss and Guy Debord's aphorism: "All revolutions go down in history, yet history does not fill up.")

## Achtung!

*DA, April 7, 1993*: When the letters dry up and
the long-distance calls cease and the world's
surprised to learn that you're still alive (but)
en route to foggy oblivion—this is the moment
to tap the cistern and to haul up long-stored
provisions.

**Daniel's Dictionary**

*Bombilation*: a humming or buzzing sound,
booming. "The bombilation of guns."
—Sir Thomas Browne

"The learned bombilations of antiquaries recorded
by Macrobius."
—Anthony Grafton

### Edmund Wilson re: Compton Mackenzie

"I imagine the idea is that imperialism,
like buggery, is a sterile assertion of power,
uncomfortable for the object."

## Death

*Frances Partridge*: "I think a great deal about death and the manner of dying . . . One can only come to terms with death by pressing forward, opening the door, and looking all around the room."

## Suggested Opening for My Biographer

"Daniel Aaron was born August 4, 1912—exactly two centuries and eight months after the birth of Frederick II (The Great) of Prussia."

"As plain as a crow's caw."

## Man's Fate

*Henry James*: "[W]e are all patronized in our turn when we are not merely neglected."

## On Being Old

*Charles Tennyson:* "Now, at 91, I am undeniably, by prevailing standards, old, though whether such an age will be considered old in 50 years' time may be doubtful. I wish I could feel that my old age is typical—but I can't . . . Most unfair of all, I find that the mere fact of having attained the age of 91 is regarded as a distinction and that I receive everywhere a consideration which my achievements in so long a life certainly do not deserve . . . Am I afraid of death? Certainly. I fear the physical moment. I hate the thought of leaving this world which I have enjoyed and still enjoy so much. I hate the thought that I may live to be a burden and a misery to those who love me. As for the 'something after death,' that seems too far away to worry about—though it can't, I suppose, be so very far."

"What does she remind me of? Watercress—
cold peas."

## Postcards

My friend Bill Bottiglia, now waiting to find out
if he has a malignant kidney, observes in a post-
card: "I await the decision of His Sacred Majesty
Chance." This phrase cropped up in the correspondence between Voltaire (Bill's specialty)
and Frederick the Great.

**Newton Arvin and
the Truman Capote Literary Trust**

The likely winners of the "Truman Capote
Award for Literary Criticism in Memory of
Newton Arvin" will be critics who probably
never heard of Newton and who have long
repudiated his critical assumptions.

## Time Warp

*Tuesday, April 19*: Time, 8:20 AM. Place, Warren House. Listening to Berlioz' *Le Corsaire*. Desk uncluttered, my office my solace and salvation where my life is stored and packaged. Not yet completely restored after my "total hip procedure" but mending steadily as the veins reconnect and the metal connecting rod in my hip nestles into flesh and bone. At odd moments I think of death and oblivion. Last Sunday I listened to a Bach cantata—"Ich steh' mit einem Fuß im Grabe"—or something like that.

## Superior

*May* 23: Opulent spring thanks to excessive rain.
The azalea bush outside the kitchen window a
marvel though perhaps over-trimmed. Americans "grieving" over death of Jacqueline Kennedy,
USA's closest approximation of "goddess." (I met
her once at a party in NYC and chatted with her
for two minutes about the Library of America.)
My essay collection out but expect nothing save
a few slurs and half-hearted commendations.
Still I feel blessed. I've never considered myself
"superior" but I've had superior chances, uplifted,
you might say, by certain privileges: an education,
exposure to books and music. I've been able to
dip into that vast cornucopia. Lucky me.

### Sir Walter Raleigh

What is our life? A play of passion.
And what our mirth but music of division?
Our mothers' wombs the tiring houses be
Where we are drest for this short comedy.
Heaven the judicious sharp spectator is
Who sits and marks what here we do amiss.
The graves that hide us from the searching sun
Are like drawn curtains when the play is done.
Thus playing post we to our latest rest,
And then we die, in earnest, not in jest.

## Utopians

*Nicholas Spice*: "They compound the misfortunes of oppression by inviting the oppressed to exchange the limited uncertainties of a miserable reality for the unlimited uncertainties of a miserable dream. And they are rarely around to pick up the pieces."

"Last Days"

Trapped between his office and his bed,
He made extended journeys in his head,
Revived embarrassed memories long dead,
Walked paths he'd vowed never to retread.

## Daniel's Dictionary

*Verbigeration:* obsessive repetition of meaningless words and phrases. (Symptom of mental illness.)

**John Williams**

*Obit*, New York Times, *Mar. 14, 1994*: And with him (a friend, indeed, who rescued me) dies a secret. Came to know him at Smith College where he was a visiting writer—a dry, funny, and large-hearted man. His novel *Stoner* (1965) my favorite of his books. It was my good fortune to have met him when I did.

**Setting Words to Music**

Can often create odd effects. Thus Nahum Tate's
lines for Purcell's *Dido and Aeneas*:

  "Our plot has took,
   The Queen's forsook"
     or
   "Thus on the fatal banke of Nile,
    Weeps the deceitful crocodile."

(Gwynne Evans recalls a line from Dryden's
adaptation of *Paradise Lost*. Eve says, "I myself
am proud of me.")

## Daniel's Dictionary

*Cumshaw*: tip, gratuity—from Chinese *gamsia*, thanks.

*Judder*: to shake rapidly, spasmodically (combines "jerk" and "shudder").

*Roborant*: (Lat. *robur/robor*: oak) restorative, strengthener, a tonic.

*Orlop*: lowest deck of a ship.

*Anemometer*: (Gk. *anemes*) instrument for measuring wind force and velocity.

*Steeve*: a spar or derrick with block at one end, used for stowing cargoes.

*Bye-blow*: bastard, result of a passing fancy.

## The Cultural Revolution, 1960

*Mary Lee Settle:* "I wonder if anyone in 1960 knew that an era was at an end. We didn't think of it. The whole complacent world was a wall to bounce opinions against while we lived in its glow. We were the Eisenhower children who stamped their feet at Daddy. We had no way to imagine lives free of that benign confinement. But what we did not bother to imagine had already begun. Quietly in the South, nice black boys with crew cuts sat at Woolworth counters in their best sports jackets while we read novels about alienation of power, and went to Martha's Vineyard. We knew people who knew the Kennedys. Our politics that year were sexual. Angry intelligence, talent rising out of poverty, and being Jewish, were tickets to our beds. We had, to them, some evasive scent of power."

## The Truelove

*Patrick O'Brian*: Stephen Maturin speaking:
". . . then it is a toss of the coin which falls first,
your hair or your teeth, your eyes or your ears;
then comes impotence, for age gelds a man
without hope or retrieve, saving him a mort
of anguish."

**Opening Paragraph of *Peter Simple***

*Frederick Marryat*: "If I cannot narrate a life of adventurous and daring exploits, fortunately I have no heavy crimes to confess; and, if I do not rise in the estimation of the reader for acts of gallantry and devotion in my country's cause, at least I may claim the merit of zealous and humble and unobtrusive continuance in my vocation. We are all of us variously gifted from Above, and he who is content to walk, instead of to run, on his allotted path through life, although he may not so rapidly attain the goal, has the advantage of not being out of breath upon his arrival. Not that I mean to infer that my life has not been one of adventure. I only mean to say that in all which has occurred, I have been a passive, rather than an active personage; and, if events of interest are to be recorded, they certainly have not been sought by me."

**Daniel's Dictionary**

*Destructive Encapsulation*: the conflating of two words, a thinning or denuding of the verbal forest. Examples: disinterested/uninterested; enormity/enormousness; titillate (to stimulate by touching lightly) and titivate (to make decorative additions, to spruce up).

**Prayer**

(After nearly being whacked by one of those
truck-like cars on Mt. Auburn.)

God be thanked for not having to believe in Him,
For diverting thunderbolts from my incredulous
     head
And nudging me away from fatal emergencies
Just in time to foil Time's contract with
     Necessity.

## Some Random Events for Cambridge Stories

In a demonized setting, the untended and unfilled potholes of Francis Avenue are sinks cunningly placed to suck in and inhale unwary cars. Description of an anguished Lexus honking for help before being enveloped in a flash of gleaming metal . . .

Incident off Brattle St.: "It was almost 10:00 AM. There was no wind, and the thermometer in the window of the barbershop registered 92 degrees. Ralph was standing on the corner of Hilliard and Mt. Auburn as Professor Bannister posted a letter. A moment later Ralph watched the old man rise slowly and quietly from the ground in the talons of an enormous owl. Ralph was very surprised. (No: make it 8:00 PM, a freezing white winter scene.)"

## The Nihilist's Revenge
### (Dictated by Brother David)

Through the window, down the rope,
The Nihilist and the maid elope.
Not a moment do they lose,
Save to stop and light the fuse.
Slowly on its path it crawls
Toward the old gray castle walls,
Past the Cossacks with their sabers
Still at rest from recent labors,
And the noble body guard,
They are snoring just as hard.

A flash! A roar! and Moscow rumbles
And the tower of Ivan tumbles.
Up sky high goes Godstad Pfouski
Ivan Rurik Romanowski,
Also little Moses Kahn
From the village of Kazan.
Vladimir and Max Pulaski,
Peter Ulric and Hydraski,

Isaac Ozam of Torique,
One Jim Bogado, a Greek,
And a soldier, Peter Henski
Of the noted Prebojenski,
Kutuseff and Fedorovitch,
Little No Account von Stovitch,
Seizendorf and Jake Zabatski,
Remanoff and Ruffonratski.

This is but the half of them,
Herr von Freitag Stobelpem,
And a Jew that sent her Rhine wine,
Moses Aaron Eiffel Einstein,
Drinkee Allee Samee Tea—
He from Hong Kong—Sam Wing Lee,
Isawwiskey and Tschenimsky,
Waronetzski and Chewbimsky—
And two svenska yentlemen,
Yohn and Ole Petersen.

**Pilgrim's Progress**

(My story. Everyone's story.)

"Here therefore they met with a very brisk lad,
that came out of that country Conceit; and his
name was *Ignorance*." (Note that he came by way
of "a little crooked lane.")

## Not Racist, Really . . .

"Jack said, 'This may sound like a racist remark, but I really do think some black faces are harder to see in the dark than most white faces.'"

## Sophicality

*DA*: "He had a deep voice and spoke with deliberation, so most people assumed he was a wise man."

**James Reston**

*Dec. 8*: James Reston, dean of reporters, died
a few days ago. The obits long and respectful.
*New York Times* story covered almost two full
pages. Frank Sinatra (now being recommended
for a Medal of Honor) wouldn't get more
space although he's more widely remembered
and deeply loved than "Scotty" Reston. And
understandably so, for though tarnished by the
company he's kept, he has pleased millions of
his countrymen—me included.

Sinatra is one or two years my junior (Surprise!),
Reston three years my senior. I met him (I think)
in the late '40s (perhaps a little later), at Charles
Page's house in Northampton. We spent several
hours drinking and talking. He and Charlie had
been athletes at the University of Illinois. Charlie
became a successful sociologist, Reston an even
more prominent journalist, if not yet a "celebrity."
He talked about the Press and misconceptions
about it, but I can't remember precisely what he
said. Relaxed, good-humored, unpretentious, he
evinced a kind of "specialness."

*Feb. 8:* The death of a popular entertainer evokes
a more spontaneous response (loving and emotional) than the deaths of most Presidents, priests,
or scientists—even famous sportsmen. A spate
of them have kicked the bucket in the last few
months. I feel the loss—and why not? We remember our delight in hearing them sing, watching
them dance and act, and the ambience we and
they shared. They are the background of our private romances, happy moments. When they die,
they carry off something of ourselves, and less of
us remain. So we rejoice for what they gave and
grieve for what they've taken away.

## *Moby Dick* in Film

The first screen version was the 1926 silent movie
*The Sea Beast*, which starred John Barrymore
and Dolores Costello. Its success led to a second,
talking version featuring Barrymore . . . with
Joan Bennett. *The Sea Beast* turned the novel
into a love story garnished by a spectacular whale
hunt, and the 1930 *Moby Dick* follows suit. Ahab
(Barrymore) is a boozing skirt-chaser who falls
in love with a preacher's daughter (Bennett). The
couple is effectively kept apart, however, by two
things: Ahab's jealously scheming brother Derek
(Lloyd Hughes), and Moby Dick, who has the dis-
courtesy to bite off Ahab's leg. All ends happily,
though, when Ahab kills the whale and gets the
girl. In the final frames, if you can picture it,
Bennett looks up at Barrymore and exclaims,
"Why, Ahab Ceely, you're crying!"

## Caricatures

*Emerson's Journals*: "Caricatures are often the truest history of the time for they only express in a pointed unequivocal action what really lies at the bottom of a great many plausible, public, hypocritical Manoeuvres."

## The Difficulty of Describing a Process

For example, how to fry a pan of fish, change
a tire, sew on a button, repair a cello—and to do
so with grace and precision. Kipling could, and
Hemingway, and Steinbeck, too, at his best. What
does it take? A sympathetic eye and ear, economy,
no fudging, no blurring, nothing tentative . . .
a Picasso drawing, a surgeon's confident incision.

## Masterpieces

A masterpiece in one form can inspire another
in a different form, musical spin-offs from
Shakespeare, for example the compositions of
Berlioz, Handel, Verdi, etc. The best adaptations
are at once a tribute and an exercise of love but
never soft and pretty. No. Rather graceful and
severe.

## Old Age

*Hugo Williams*: "As we get older, natural change seems to be dropping bigger and bigger hints about our own dissolution, so naturally we fight back. As we get weaker, we have to side with ourselves more, to make it fairer. Again and again we reach for the word 'strange' to describe what is going on, only to realize that it is we who are strange."

## Death Notices

"To the members of the Faculty of Arts and Sciences: With great regret, I inform you of the death of . . ." These notifications seem to arrive several times a week, reminders to the Emeriti that they too are paltry things who will soon be memorialized on a white card edged in black. I cut these cards in half and cover them with shopping lists.

## Thought for the Day

I've not become a "history" in the sense that
Goethe said he had become (that is, in its most
flattering sense, so famous that he hardened in
his lifetime, long before his death, into an icon)
but still I am a "history," an artifact of history,
of time. My very longevity is "historical," because
old people like me are physically and perhaps
mentally the consequences of the first twenty
years of their lives, of their nutrition and education. I am a ringed tree. The postmortemists
scrutinizing my corpse will be "identifying the
aging of a human body" but also "tracing the
social history of a century" (Raymond Tallis).
What is "historical" about me is the totality of
my nurturing—the food I consumed, my physical
activity from early childhood to now, my physical
and mental exercise.

So one could write a physiological autobiography,
I suppose, replete with family medical records as
far back as possible; hygienic accidents, physical
exploits; smoking, drinking. This information
would be arranged and correlated with the
medical practices and theories prevailing during
the subject's life. The autobiographer would also
record his social and intellectual development,
information related to his psychological makeup,

his aesthetic views, sexual attitudes and history, dreams, and his thoughts and theories about death and aging.

## A Western Journey with Mr. Emerson

RWE on Mormonism: "[I]t's an after-clap of Puritanism."

"And then the Indians, although destitute of beards, had hair that was like horsehair,—heavy, long, coarse, black, lying thick about their heads, and held in their teeth sometimes to keep it still."

J.B. Thayer and RWE visit the Chinese theater in San Francisco to survey "their theater and gambling-houses, opium dens, restaurants, and Joss-houses . . . The Chinese opium-dens were fearful things: 'There is not much aspiration there,—or inspiration', said Mr. Emerson as our party came out; and he expressed his wonder at the strange way in which our civilization seems to fail to take hold of these people, and at their persistence in herding and huddling together, where there was such vast room all about them."

RWE "generally smoked a single cigar after our mid-day dinner, or after tea, and occasionally after both."

RWE on Redwood trees: "'These trees,' said Mr. Emerson, 'have a monstrous talent for being tall.'"

## Henry James re: His Visit to Étretat

French women on the bathing beach: "A majestic plumpness flourished all around me—the plumpness of triple chins and deeply dimpled hands . . . It was the corpulence of ladies who are thoroughly well fed, and who never walk a step that they can spare." These ladies contrasted to their American counterparts: "The assiduity with which the women of America measure the length of our democratic pavements is doubtless a factor in their frequent absence of redundancy of outline."

"Conformists"

Paper cups in hand,
Wired to the same Drummer,
March loud bands of youth.

"Success"

Not long after his shame
He became a "Name,"
And thanks to his bruited "Sin"
Moved back from "Out" to "In."

## New Year's Eve, 1999

Deaths of longtime acquaintances C. Vann
Woodward, whom I first met umpty-um years
ago at one of those small & genial meetings
of the Southern Historical Society (where all
sectional bitterness dissolved in bourbon), and
Elliot Richardson with whom I served on the
Board of Salzburg Seminar and kept in touch
with thereafter, the only Republican office-
holder I supported. Both were men of conservative temper, men of honor & quintessentially
of their respective sections.

I didn't think I could live this long, impossibly
distant when I began to think of futurity. And
it is a long time between 2000 and 1912. If you
think of history as a train ride through familiar
if ever-changing landscape, I've been a passenger
for close to 90 years, missing most of the scenery
but halted at points in the journey and given
the opportunity to look around. Had I been less
self-centered and more curious and detached,
I would have had a denser story to tell. Still, I like
the image of one's human span as a train ride
(note: not a journey, not a search, not extra-
natural). At a never recoverable point, you find
yourself on that train. You ride and ride and get
to know some of the passengers encountered on
what used to be known as the Observation Car.
(That figure or object seems appropriate to me,
because my first vivid encounter with Life-
Reality was on the train ride from Chicago to
Los Angeles in 1917 with my parents and siblings.
That train ride and others to follow were correl-
atives of domestic instability.) During this long
trip, there are many hellos and good-byes, some
epiphanic, some wrenching, but most unintense.
Not many people worship at the altar of the
dead. Time is less an anodyne than a narcotic.
I imagine my end at a train stop. I put on my coat

(the night will be wet and foggy) and pick up my suitcase, a small one, and smile at passengers who haven't yet arrived at their destinations, and step across the empty platform.

## Correspondence

I liken the reading through fifty years of correspondence (alphabetized) to the experience of
sitting in blackness in an empty theater, the
stage ablaze in white light. Streaming across it
a procession of men and women, some familiar,
some hardly recognizable or totally forgotten.
Occasionally, one of the figures stops and glowers
reproachfully at me hiding in the darkness, but
most are indifferent and empty-eyed. I am uncomfortable, feeling more guilty than puzzled.
Emotions long squelched flow through me.
The past never recaptured—only encountered—
friends, lovers, petitioners.

## Jewish Honor

Found this scribbled in a note—written sometime
in 1999: Why Jews are honored and despised.
What is "honored" is their history & durability,
what is embedded in the Old Testament Hebrews,
passionate guardians of the Sacred Word but
marginal to the marginal business of quotidian
life. (The Jews admired by poets & philosophers
are the stargazers, loners. See Santayana's comment on Spinoza, the only kind of Jew he could
stomach, the separate isolated Jew.)

Jews fare better in large, imperial, heteroge-
neous societies where earlier tribal loyalties &
customs and isolations have blurred. Hence they
tend to flourish in capitalist cultures shaped in
part by abstract and international economic
forces. They take root in small communities as
well, but in Europe (not necessarily in the U.S.)
they are a distinctive minority and are made to
feel different. Their histories, social conditions,
aptitudes, networks, language (Yiddish) enable
a sizable number of them to succeed econom-
ically if not politically. Because they aren't
"rooted," they are easily turned over and up and
under; and they know how to replant themselves
precisely because they aren't stuck to any one
place or society or system (like the gypsies). They

survive—and are useful or supply some service in any kind of society or system—which makes them more dangerous and detestable to their persecutors. At times their only course is protective mimicry. Jews are still at risk everywhere, if less so in U.S. or in Anglo-secular societies. For all the talk to the contrary, free-thinking Jews have been anathema to priesthoods—including the Jewish.

Old Jewish radicals blamed capitalism for the persistence of persecution, but abstract capitalism (if not individual capitalists) has augmented the economics that weaken (and in some instances obliterated) tribal faiths that buttressed powerful religions.

Recognizing the truth of clichés about impetuosity of youth, rushing from point to point, living for the moment. Age tantamount to slowing down as expectations falter, reflective pauses more frequent, increasing tiredness of the will. Youth: life a highway with whizzing cars, emergency stops only (accidents or when passengers have to pee). Old Age: out of traffic, out of the blur of speed. Time to study a leaf, a petal, a tree.

## GOD

Fusion of Eye, Hand, Blood, Muscle, Heart,
Sound, Color plus a whiff of the Unknown.

"Blame"

You can't be blamed
For being you.
No! Blame THEM,
And blame the TIMES
That baked and shaped you.
And if you cheat and trim—
Blame HIM.

DA is five months away from start of his 96th
year. He is far from elation but not depressed.
Accidents, crumblings, mental brittleness of last
months not encouraging, but Old Age is neither
Yeats' "paltry thing" nor May Time either. I wince
at all the clichés (viz., "Old Age isn't for sissies,"
etc.), and all the self-encouragements and boast-
ing in the claque of the elders. It's Henley-esque
"captain of my soul" stuff.

### Daniel's *Pomes*

Boys?
Hobbledehoys—
No music in their talk.

Girls?
Booted look-alikes,
Holding their heads like banners,
Wearing concessionary smiles.

## Nostromo/Costaguana

Portrait of a dictator. Caricature of a military
bravo in a Mexican newspaper—composite of a
rogue peasant, mustachios, curved beak of a nose,
enormous spurs, the "atrocious grotesqueness,"
the "imbecile and dominating stare," the "mass
of gold on sleeves and breast."

"The popular mind is incapable of skepticism; and
that incapacity delivers their helpless strength
to the wiles of swindlers, and to the pitiless
enthusiasms of leaders inspired by visions of high
destiny."

Note: Like Hawthorne, Conrad points out that
only a stick was necessary to club a person to
death. No elaborate machine required for that
simple task.

## On the Grasshopper

*Peter Milward*, The Secret Life of Insects: "Even in his ephemerality he grasps eternity, in what T. S. Eliot calls 'the timeless moment' . . . In a word, he stands for the famous definition of eternity proposed by Boethius, 'The total, simultaneous and perfect possession of unlimited life.'"

## Some Thoughts on Dashiell Hammett & the Continental "Op"

His crime stories of the 1920s & 1930s, rich-textured, "realistic" fantasies, gorgeous and tawdry, terse, tough, and—above all—mannered. Aimed at the "Spicy-Detective" crowd S. J. Perelman joked about. Sometimes Tough-Guy language witty and funny. Influence on Hemingway? Perhaps. (The terse & laconic is also a strain in American "costumed" writing. DH's Crime Characters have ingenious names. Compare Stephen Crane, O. Henry, Frank L. Packard.) They speak an unreal patois and live in a world of cartoon-people, moldy or muscled, and have names like Burke Pangburn, Leopold Gantvoort, Harvey Gatewood.

DH's tough Ops "light up Fatimas." Eyes are giveaways in his stories, especially eyes that are too closely set or of "an indistinct color." His stories often begin with a dramatic event and grow complicated as new characters and additional information muddle the action. New deaths and mayhem. Then the big dramatic scene and gathering of loose ends: the narrative is retold with the missing facts now supplied—and sometimes a coda. The characters have no characters. They are points on a chart, dressed-up dummies and interchangeable. The only thing "real" in the stories are the descriptions of streets and buildings and articles of clothing. Plots are urban fairy stories, characters all out of proportion: giants, midgets, freaks plumped down in hotel lobbies, offices, mansions.

## Memorial to JSA

When we bought the Cummington house in
the early '60s, I think she felt that she'd finally
reached Home, although she had imposed
herself in Cambridge, Northampton, Wellfleet
(wherever we lived) in our various dwellings.
The Cummington house was her Great Good
Place—old, not too large or small, plenty of land,
open and yet sheltered by maples that seemed to
grow taller and denser every year. It was close to
Northampton and yet somehow remote from it.
It was a safe place for children & dogs & cats.
The only troublesome animals about were por-
cupines even though we had made the porcupine
a house-totem after a huge one had been shot
inside it just before we moved in and we had
tried to placate its spirit in a ritual fire.

JSA liked company (selected) from anywhere,
and she liked to be alone. She managed to keep
the house homely and elegant in a very special
way. She could be a good & inventive cook, and
she excelled at July 4 parties where locals, friends
from nearby places, and foreign visitors ate and
drank with much satisfaction.

JSA could be a solicitous, generous, warmhearted friend—and a blunt and outspoken one. Some time ago she bought a space in the Cummington graveyard for both of us.

## Etymology

*Richard Chenevix Trench*, On the Study of Words: An exercise in piety. "And one of the arts of a great poet or prose writer, who wishes to add emphasis to his style, to bring out all the latent forces of his native tongue, will often consist in reconnecting a word by his use of it with its original derivation, in not suffering it to forget itself and its father's house, though it would."

*Michiko Kakutani*, New York Times, *May 18*:
"In another chapter, Mr. Helprin rails against
'mouth-breathing morons in backwards baseball
caps and pants that fall down; Slurpee-sucking
geeks who seldom see daylight; pretentious and
earnest hipsters who want you to wear bamboo
socks so the world won't end; women who have
lizard tattoos winding from the navel to the nape
of the neck; beer-drinking dufuses who pay to
watch noisy cars driving around in a circle for
eight hours at a stretch; and to an entire race of
females, now entering middle age, that speaks in
North American Chipmunk and seldom makes
a statement without, like, a question mark at
the end?'"

## Plagiarism (Lat. *plagiarius*, kidnapper, from *plaga*, snare/net)

*Robert Musil*: Plagiarism can be direct stealing or disguised stealing or more abstract forms of thievery hard to detect because they leave no tangible evidence and have dissolved into essence. "When one leans against a wall one's suit ends up all covered in patches of white wax—without plagiarism being involved."

## My Fellow Men

Crossing the Yard every day, I mingle with the parade of look-alikes similarly dressed. They carry coffee-filled paper cups, their eyes glued to cell phones. I am a remnant of a dead civilization. Darwin (whose biography by Janet Browne I'm currently steeped in) was shaken at the sight of Tierra Fuegians he encountered in Patagonia, because he knew that he belonged to the same species. And I know that I'm a member of the great family of Vandals who make up a good part of the Swinish Multitude and desecrate the landscape but who also can be good-natured and helpful and kind.

## Sports at Harvard (1906), Interview with Charles W. Eliot, Harvard President

"To discontinue football, hockey, and basket ball at Harvard would do no harm," he said. "Basket ball is very objectionable. It is too rough, and there are too many chances for cheating. The rules have been stretched so that they spoil the game. It would be a good thing especially to have basket ball discontinued."

In discussing other forms of sports President Eliot admitted that, as baseball was so popular, he would not advocate its abolition, notwithstanding the objections to it. Hockey he stamped as too rough.

"It requires team work. And I must say I have no use for a game that requires that . . . It is not open enough, and as in basket ball, its rules have been distorted. Rowing and tennis are the only sports in which honorable play altogether is practiced. You can no more cheat in those two sports than in a game of cards; you would be crowded out of society if you tried."

**Review of Cecil B. DeMille's film "Cleopatra" which appeared in the *Manchurian Daily News,* "The Oldest English Language Newspaper in Manchuria," published in Dairen.**

GRAMOROUS AND FLAGRANT
CLEOPATRA BRISTLES EYES

So extravagance, so lavishly, so fanciest betimes, Cecil B. DeMille's "Cleopatra" will be shown to the fans from January 7, Monday, at the Nikka-tsu-kan cinema hall.

Cecil B. DeMille in "Cleopatra" produced a eye-bristling spectacles classed among the most thrillings of last year's screens givings.

The critic is certain several superfluous word of praises can be offered to this picture which is so colossal, so charming and so vividly with an eye to interesting, and that is ahead of his expectations. But eyeing from artistic points, this is just to get the passing mark, to boots.

"Cleopatra" Is Lavishness.

All that "Cleopatra" possesses is lavishness not only, but also it contains some fine acting, especiary in part of gramorous, flagrant and competent Claudette Colbert, who makes the roll as Cleopatra every inch, an ell.

"Cleopatra" is the luring picture-scroll entracing romance of the Siren of the Nile and the inflexible and valiant Roman of them all.

The "Cleopatra" the critic sees here is not so immoral woman of the vampireship type as the critic has been taught from his teacher, but rather beautiful martry who intended to saying Egypt and a woman whom we can easily entertain with friendly sentiments. This "Cleopatra" at any rate is one of those breathtaking spectacles which seems able to direct and to review.

It is said that the film costs at a million and a half dollars and in which more than 5,000 persons are to produce.

### Story Well Cranked.

The story is cranked from a scene of struggle of power between Cleopatra and his brother, Ptolemy, in Egypt.

The critic has no space to hear repetition in these columns that the content of Cleopatra is too popular to insist it. You, the fans, certainly be struck all of a hump if you see the Demille for sets of several thrilling scenes of battle on the sands and in the sea, the Egyptian armies fighting against the romans, and of dancing by the Egyptian girls who swing and swirl and revolving through grand marble halls and on the sumptuous barge to the swish of gully slaves.

## Petunias

At the end of Farwell Place, just as it turns into
the walk that divides Christ Church from the
Cambridge graveyard, you can see a clump of
volunteer Petunias, tiny blue flowers modest
and winsome. I think what a silly name for such
lovely things. I check my dictionary. "Petunia"
derives from the obsolete French word *petun*
(tobacco), which in turn comes from the Por-
tuguese *petum* which is based on a word in the
language of the Tupi-Guarani (South American).

So my dislike of the word disappears.

**For DA's "Wonderland"**

"Twinkle, twinkle blinky star.
 Do you know how far you are?"
"I'm not sure, but let me guess:
 Thirty light years, more or less?"

**Daniel Aaron** is Professor Emeritus of English and American Literature at Harvard University and cofounder of The Library of America. Among his books are *Men of Good Hope: A Story of American Progressives* (1951), *Writers on the Left: Episodes in American Literary Communism* (1961), *The Unwritten War: American Writers and the Civil War* (1973), *American Notes: Selected Essays* (1994), and his memoir, *The Americanist* (2007). Aaron began keeping commonplace books in 1933 and, as of 2015, attends to them still.

And on the seventh day . . . Black Sabbath circa 1970. L–r: Terry 'Geezer' Butler; Bill Ward; John 'Ozzy' Osbourne; Tony Iommi.

'Smoke it! Get high!' The band plus rubber friend, London 1971.

Four men in a leaky boat, on the Hudson River, New York 1971.

Like punk is not about to happen. Madison Square Garden, December 1976.

The last New York show by the original line-up, Madison Square Garden, August 27 1978. Within months, Tony Iommi had announced he could no longer work with Ozzy.

'Without my wife I'd have been a hot dog salesman.'
Ozzy with manager – and soon to be wife –
Sharon Osbourne (née Arden), March 1982.

July 13 1985. JFK Stadium, Philadelphia. The temporarily
reunited Sabbath line-up about to go onstage at Live Aid.
'We're gonna do "Food Glorious Food",' Ozzy told reporters.

Killing yourself to live. In every hotel, Tony would have blankets draped across the windows. Black candles would be burning and gallons of iced-orange would be in the refrigerator, next to metal boxes filled with

Ozzy onstage with Sabbath again at the 2001 Ozzfest, in America. By now an almost annual occurrence.